A HISTORY OF FREEMASONRY IN WILTSHIRE
HASTINGS GOLDNEY

─·─ ─·─ ─·─ ─·─ ─·─ ─·─ ─·─ ─·─

A HISTOKY OF FREEMASONRY IN WILT-SHIRE

A HISTOEY OF FEEEMASONEY

IN

WILTSHIRE

INCLUDING

AN ACCOUNT OF THE PROVINCIAL GRAND LODGE AND ITS

SUBORDINATE LODGES, AND A ROLL OF THE GRAND

OFFICERS OF THE PROVINCE, AND LISTS OF THE

WORSHIPFUL MASTERS OF THE SEVERAL LODGES

AND ALSO

AN ACCOUNT OF THE PROVINCIAL GRAND ROYAL ARCH CHAPTER

AND ITS DEPENDENT CHAPTERS, AND A ROLL OF THE

GRAND OFFICERS OF THE PROVINCE, AND LISTS

OF THE PRINCIPALS OF THE SEVERAL CHAPTERS

BY

FREDERICK HASTINGS GOLDNEY

PAST GRAND STEWARD OF ENGLAND GRAND TREASURER AND SENIOR GRAND WARDEN OF WILTS

ETC., ETC., ETC.

"Audi, vide, tace."

FOR PRESENTATION ONLY

LONDON: PRINTED BY VIRTUE AND CO., LIMITED, CITY ROAD.

THE EIGHT HON. LOED METHUEN, THE R.W. PROVINCIAL GRAND MASTER FOR WILTSHIRE.

My Loud,

To no one can this small work be so properly addressed as to yourself, who devoted so much of your time and influ-ence to promoting Freemasonry in Wilt-shire whilst in its decadence, and who, since its revival, have in so large a mea-sure extended your generous patronage to its many objects.

The importance of the subject of this History is undeniable, and it naturally claims the patronage of one under whose rule Freemasonry in Wiltshire has resumed its ancient spirit and lustre, has increased its numbers from tens to hundreds, and quadrupled its lodges— landmarks as they are in the Order, which must for all time distinguish the happy period during which your Lord-ship has presided over this Province, and proofs of the necessary effects of a revival of strict discipline combined with an unbiassed regard to merit and long service.

With the belief that this my humble offering towards the increase of Mason-ic lore will not be found to contain any-thing repugnant to truth and tradition, nor yet to disclose any of the mysteries and secrets of our Order, or the private affairs of lodges and the brethren, I ven-ture to hope that your Lordship will be disposed to look with a not too critical severity upon its faults and deficiencies.

Sincerely trusting that your life, so beneficial to Freemasonry, may long be preserved to the great advantage of the Province of Wiltshire as well as of the Craft generally, and with the profound-est respect and regard, I beg to sub-scribe myself

Tour Lordship's most obedient Servant and most humble Brother,

FKEDEKICK HASTINGS GOLDNEY,

Grand Treasurer and

Senior Grand Warden of Wilts.

Kowtden House, Chippenham,

St. John's Day, 1880.

CONTENTS.

PAGE

HISTORY OF FREEMASONRY IN WILTSHIRE.

TT is not intended in this brief History of Free--masonry in the Province of Wilts to enter upon any general disquisition as to the condition, numbers, or influence of the craft in the present day; still less to repeat what others have said of the origin, history, and antiquity of Freemasonry. The following pages are put forth simply with the view of increasing the interest of the brethren in Masonry in general, and in their own Province and individual lodges in particular; and it is, therefore, earnestly hoped that the imperfections and shortcomings of this slight record of former times will be looked upon by its readers with fraternal indulgence.

The various facts and particulars have been gleaned by researches made through a wide though somewhat unfruitful field, and are offered as a small contribution to the knowledge of an interesting subject in the hope that others may be induced to add to it, and to increase our information by bringing to light many memorials of Masonry now lying in obscurity.

Care has been taken to avoid disclosing any of the secrets of our art, and the private concerns of the different lodges referred to and their members, so that any one seeking in these pages for the discovery of them will be disappointed, and cannot do better than find consolation in the sage remarks of H.E.H. the late Prince Albert in the following letter, published in Sir Theodore Martin's "Life of the Prince Consort: "—

"I will get Alice to read to me the article about Freemasons. It is not likely to contain the whole secret. The circumstance which provokes you only into finding fault with the Order, viz., that husbands dare not communicate the secret of it to their wives, is just one of its best features. If to be able to be silent is one of the chief virtues of the husband, then the test which puts him in opposition to that being towards whom he constantly shows the greatest weakness is the hardest of all, and therefore the most compendious of virtues; and the wife should not only rejoice to see him capable of withstanding such a test, but should take occasion out of it to vie with him in virtue by taming the inborn curiosity which she inherits from her mother Eve,"

The historical data of the lodges of this Province are few, and it must be admitted also that the amount of information with regard to their members is scanty as compared with the interest of the subject. This is partly to be accounted for by there not having been any accurate record of provincial lodges kept amongst the books of the Grand Lodge until after the union of the two Grand Lodges in 1813, and also to there not having been any central depository for' the old minute-books, accountbooks, and documents of the provincial lodges; so that these books when filled up, or when a lodge was removed or discontinued, were left in the hands of the Secretary or Worshipful Master for the time being, and were afterwards no doubt lost or destroyed. It is hoped, however, that there may still be ancient minutebooks and records in existence, whose discovery may enable many a gap to be filled up and missing link supplied, so that the Masonic spirit in this Province may be traced back to remoter times, and the longforgotten acts of our forefathers in the craft brought back to remembrance.

Though England was not divided into Provinces until. 1727, there had undoubtedly been lodges throughout the country in direct communication with the Grand Lodge from a much earlier period, but there are not any records of them in this county; for the earliest lodge minutes which have been discovered commence in 1732, whilst others commence in 1792, 1794, and 1817, and the remainder are of a still later date.

The first mention of a Provincial Grand Lodge for Wiltshire is contained in the rough minutes of a Provincial Grand Lodge held at Salisbury in 1777, found amongst the Masonic papers of Brother Michael Burrough, of Salisbury (the writer's great-grandfather), who was Grand Secretary of this Province more than a century ago, and was also Grand Superintendent of Eoyal Arch Masonry for this County, and the first Grand Master for Wiltshire of the Knights Templar on the reorganization of that Order.

The following letter from the Secretary of the Grand Lodge shuts out all hope of information regarding early times from the source whence it could have been most naturally expected; and the writer's subsequent exhaustive personal search, with the courteous assistance of Brother Hervey, G.S., and the Librarian, amongst the Grand Lodge records at Freemasons' Hall confirmed the fact that there was nothing to be found in that quarter illustrative of the early history of Freemasonry in Wiltshire.

"Freemasons' Hall, London, W.C.

"*September Hat,* 1877.

"Dear Sir and Brother,

"I am in receipt of your letter of the 17th inst., and regret that I can afford you very little information as regards either the Province or its lodges.

"At the union in 1813, there appear to have teen six lodges in Wiltshire, which number was increased to nine in 1825. Before that year I cannot find any record of a P.G. Master for Wilts, hut in that year a brother, J. K. Grosett, was appointed, of whom I know nothing further than thathis rule was not very beneficial to the Province, as in 1847 the number of lodges had diminished to four, and in 1853 to three.

"From 1847 to 1853 there was no P. G. Master, but on March 2nd of the latter year Lord Methuen was appointed, and by the joint exertions of his lordship and his deputy, the present Sir Daniel Gooch, the number of lodges had more than doubled by 1860, seven appearing to be in the calendar for that year.

"The present number is ten, which you of course know as well as I do.

"I am sorry that the information I can give is so meagre.

"Yours truly and fraternally,

"john Hervey, G.S.

"F. H. Goldney, Esq."

In 1732 a lodge was constituted at Salisbury under the seal of the Eight Hon. Lord Montague, the Grand Master, which rapidly increased in numbers and importance, and from its minute-books are derived the only particulars at present known of Freemasonry in Wiltshire for nearly half a century from that time. The Duke of Eichmond and the Hon. Mr. Fox were present at a meeting in the following year, and visitors of more or less distinction from London lodges appear to have been constant attendants, and in 1766 the Grand Master himself (Lord Blayney) attended the lodge and was received with special honours.

In 1769 a scheme "for the incorporation of Masons" was sent by the Grand Lodge for the consideration of the Salisbury Brethren, and the sense of their lodge thereon was by Order of the Grand Master to be transmitted to the Grand Lodge as soon as possible; but it does not seem to have met with much favour, and was allowed to be dropped. At that time the Grand Lodge had no permanent lodge-room, but met at the Horn Tavern in Meet Street, the-Crown and Anchor Tavern in the Strand, or elsewhere in London.

England was divided into Provinces under the rule of Provincial Grand Lodges in 1727, but half a century elapsed before the constitution of the Province of Wiltshire; for though in 1775 a formal request was made by the Salisbury Lodge to Brother Eobert Cooper to accept the office of Provincial Grand Master for the County (which honour he declined), it was not till 1777 that Brother Thomas Dunckerley, the P.G.M. for Dorsetshire, was appointed P.G.M. for Wilts.

The first Grand Lodge of this Province of which we have any account was, as before stated, held at Salisbury in 1777, and the following is a copy of the rough minutes of the proceedings:—

"City Of Salisbury, *September 22nd,* 1777. "A Provincial Grand Lodge for Wiltshire was opened in ample form. *Present.*

The Most Worshipful Thomas Dunckerley, Esq., P.G.M.

,, Worshipful Hugh Skeats, D.P.G.M.

,, Worshipful Jos. Hodgson, P.G.S.W.

,, Worshipful J. Edgar, jun., P.G.J.W.

,, Worshipful Jas. Wilkinson, P.G.T.

,, Worshipful Mich. Burrough, P.G.S.

,, Worshipful T. Shuttle-worth, P.G.S.B.

P.G. Stewards.

John Norton.

Wm. Chubb.

Alex. Minty.

Wm. Weeks.

Geo. Scandover.

D. N. Keele.

P.G. Tyler—G. Brown. "The Master Officers and Brethren of Salisbury Lodge, No. 47. "The Lodge at Crown, Devizes, was called, and no one appeared.

"Bight Hon. Lord Charles Montague, P.G.M. for Hants, with six of his officers.

"Six brethren from No., at Ringwood. Four brethren from No., at Blandford, and three from lodges in London, being in all No. on the occasion.

"The Salisbury Lodge paid two guineas for the Hall, and one for the fund of Charity.

"The P.G.M. recommended that no Mason be made in future for less than three guineas in this county.

"The brethren dined in open lodge, and in the evening the lodge was closed in due form and time.

"The Most Worshipful took occasion to observe that an assembly had lately been formed in S. of persons who call themselves Antient Masons, and pretend to derive an authority from D. Athol. He informed the lodge that the D. had disclaimed any knowledge of or connection with persons acting under that sanction, and that the meetings of such are so inconsistent with the principles of Freemasonry, that they had been publicly reprobated by the Grand Lodge, and that it was his wish that the Wiltshire brethren would by no means countenance their proceedings, but rather that they should give a public denial of what that assembly had asserted relative to the patronage of the D. Athol. "

On the same paper is the following memorandum of apparently other visitors at that lodge:— *Visiting Brethren.*

"Charles Wren, Esq., grandson to that celebrated G.M. Arch., the late Sir Christopher "Wren, who built St. Paul's. "— Savage, Esq., late Chief Justice of Carolina. "— Lucas, Esq., and several of his Grand Officers."

From the above it will be seen that there were at that time probably but two working lodges in the Province: the Salisbury Lodge, No. 47, and a lodge held at the Crown Inn, Devizes.

It should be observed that most of the early lodges possessed no distinctive title beyond that of the inn or tavern where they met, and also that the calendar numbers of the several lodges were from time to time altered in the books of the Grand Lodge as they became extinct by the voluntary delivering up or compulsory suspension of Warrants, or by erasure, or by dissolution through want of sufficient members. Such alterations of numbers by closing up the gaps took place in 1740, 1756, 1781, 1792, and 1863. Thus what at first sight appears in some instances to be a succession of lodges is, in fact, but a continuation of the same one.

Confusion is also caused by the spurious lodges which existed in addition to the regular ones, and those deriving authority from the Duke of Athol. One such spurious lodge was held at Devizes in 1793.

During 1777 a lengthy dispute was carried on between the Salisbury Lodge and the Grand Lodge in London, on account of the former declining to entertain the application from the Grand Lodge for a contribution towards building and furnishing their new hall, alleging the great expense they had recently been put to in building and furnishing their own lodge-room at Salisbury. The lodge was in consequence suspended, but shortly afterwards a compromise was effected, and it was reinstated on an undertaking being given to pay for the future to the Grand Lodge 5s. for every person thereafter to be made a Mason in the lodge.

From the mention of the various Counties out of which men came to be "made " in the Salisbury Lodge, one would gather that country lodges were then few and far between, or that this was an extremely popular one; yet, in 1802, the lodge was again erased on account of its members refusing to comply with the demand of the Grand Lodge, directing 2s. per annum to be paid by every member of a lodge towards "liquidating the debts of the Society;" but it appears to have gone on working and making Masons notwithstanding the erasure.

On the 25th October, 1809, this lodge, together with lodges from neighbouring Counties, went in procession, attended by the Corporation of the City, to the Cathedral, on the occasion of a special service to commemorate the fiftieth anniversary of his Majesty's accession.

At a meeting of the Grand Lodge at Freemasons' Hall on the 8th of April, 1778, under the presidency of the Duke of Manchester as Grand Master, it is recorded that, "On the complaint of Brother Dunckerley superintending over the lodges in "Wiltshire and Dorsetshire, the lodge held at Devizes was struck out of the list for contempt."

This is the last official notice of Brother Dunckerley, though he was still P.G.M. in 1787, as appears from a letter to him from Brother Michael Burrough, in which reference is made to the Salisbury Lodge.

Brother John Dainton was P.G.M. in 1792, but there is no information to be found as to his appointment.

Masonry seems to have maintained its hold upon Devizes despite the erasure of the lodge, for in addition to the Travelling Lodge, No. 170, attached to the 3rd Eegiment then quartered there (in which civilians were "made," but without any connection with the Provincial Grand Lodge), there was the Devizes Lodge, No. 270, under the constitution of the "Ancient" or "Atholl" Grand Lodge, which received the Provincial Grand Lodge in 1792.

This latter lodge, No. 270, held frequent meetings, sometimes as often as four in a month, at one of which "a recommendation was granted to brethren to obtain the degree of Holy Arch;" the number of its members rapidly increased, and it continued in full working order until it broke up, and the furniture and regalia were dispersed, in 1826.

One of its members, Brother Thomas Burrough Smith, in 1817, invited the brethren to attend a lodge at Melksham that he was about to open there, namely, the Lodge of Eectitude, which had been suspended at Westbury.

There is in the possession of Brother T. Prideaux Saunders the Warrant for the constitution of a lodge at Bradford-on-Avon, under the title of the Lodge of Unity and Friendship, which was in 1794 granted by the Earl of Moira as Acting Grand Master, under the authority of H.E.H. the Prince of Wales, G.M.

The wax impression of the seal of this Bradford Lodge is also in the possession of the same brother, as well as several copper-plate forms for certificates.

Nothing further can at present be found about this lodge except references to visitors from it entered in the minute-books of other lodges, down to the year 1823. In 1817, and subsequently, the number of the lodge was 564.

The Lodge of Eectitude is the earliest of the existing lodges of which we have consecutive minutes for each year down to the present time. They commence in 1817, when the Lodge was resumed at Melksham by permission of the Grand Lodge after its suspension at Westbury.

In 1818 a petition was presented for a Warrant of constitution for a new lodge, to be called the Lodge of Emulation, to be held at the Goddard Arms Inn, at Swindon, and the applicants were:—

John Sheppard, m Tree Inn, Devizes, No. 341.

Wm. Morse Crowdy, Foundation Lodge, Abingdon, No. 121.

Robert Withers, Lodge of Virtue, Bath, No. 311.

John Wyatt, Elm Tree Inn, Devizes, No. 341.

Samuel Sheppard,,, ,, ,,

John Osborne, ,, ,, ,,

William Gerring, Foundation Lodge, Abingdon, No. 121.

In accordance with the petition a dispensation for holding a lodge was granted, followed by the Warrant of constitution, signed by H.E.H. the Duke of Sussex, G.M.

A Eoyal Arch Chapter and Knights Templar Encampment were shortly afterwards attached to the lodge.

The earlier minute-books of this lodge are missing, and those in existence do not commence until 1852.

From an old Provincial Grand Lodge treasurer's-book, kindly given to the writer by Sir Daniel Gooch with other interesting documents, there seem to have been in 1827 four lodges belonging to this Province, which afterwards disappeared, namely:—

Lodge of Loyalty, No. 356, held at Marlborough, having 18 members. Lodge of Honour and Morality, No. 592, held at Hindon, having 16 members. Lodge of Temperance and Morality, No. 621, held at Market Lavington, having 33 members. Lodge of Union, No. 819, held at New Sarum, having 18 members. There were also the Lodge of Unity and Friendship, No. 564, held at Bradford, having 7 members, and Lodge of Eectitude, No. 639, held at Box, having 10 members, which are still in existence.

Brother John Dainton was P.G.M. in 1792, when Provincial Grand Lodge met at Devizes, but there are no records of his holding any other Provincial Grand Lodge, or of his resignation of office; but from the agitation which was commenced in 1823 for the filling up of the office of P.G.M., it is presumable that it had become vacant for some time previously.

The following letter from Brother Lacy of the Salisbury Lodge to the W.M. of the Devizes Lodge shows the feeling on the subject at that period:—

"Salisbury, *December 23rd,* 1823.

"Worshipful Sir and Brother,

"The neglect which the Province of "Wilts has experienced in having been for so many years without a Provincial Grand Master cannot have escaped the notice of yourself and your lodge.

"To a zealous Mason nothing can be more distressing than to see the art sinking into nothing for want of a helping hand to cheer and support it, and I have for some time laboured in vain to obtain for us that countenance and patronage which we are equally entitled to with other provinces, and which I think we have a right to demand. Promise after promise has been made to me by our M.W.G.M. that he would appoint a P.G.M., but hitherto without effect. The advantages of such an appointment are too obvious to need one word of comment. I therefore hasten to the object of my addressing you, which is to communicate to you a resolution entered into by the Lodge of the Five Alls, over which I have the honour to preside, expressing its high sense of the benefits the Province would receive by the appointment of a P.G.M., and suggesting the probability there would be of obtaining so desired an object by the united efforts of all the lodges of the Province.

"With this view I beg to request the favour of your communicating with your brothers upon the expediency of appointing a meeting at some central

place in the county where the masters of each lodge may attend, deputed by their respective lodges to draw up a respectful but earnest petition to H.R.H. the Duke of Sussex, that he would not withhold from us the privileges which he so graciously extends to other provinces.

"If the plan be approved of, I shall have much pleasure in receiving your opinion and that of your brethren upon the subject. Perhaps Devizes would be the best and most convenient spot for assembling, and I take the liberty of suggesting whether Wednesday, the 28th of January next, may be fixed as the day of meeting. "I am, W. Sir and Brother,

"Yours very fraternally,

"Jas. Lacy, Jun.

"To the W. Master of the Lodge of Freemasons, Devizes."

The agitation ended in the appointment of Brother John Eock Grosett, M.P. for Chippenham, as P.G.M. in 1825. He was installed at Marlborough, but in consequence of some informality he was again installed at a special lodge held at Kensington Palace for the installation of Provincial Grand Masters, over which H.E.H. the Duke of Sussex, G.M. , presided. The official announcement of the appointment was given by the following letters from the joint Grand Secretaries, and from the P.G.M.:—

"Freemasons' Hall, London, *Augmt 23rd,* 1825. "W. Master,

"We have to acquaint you that the M. W. Grand Master has been pleased to appoint J. R. Grosett, Esq., M.P., of Lacock Abbey, Provincial Grand Master for the county of Wilts, to whom therefore you will in future address all your communications relating to the craft, except your returns and applications for certificates, which are to be made direct to us, in conformity with the laws of the limited Grand Lodge, page 72, Book of Constitutions.

"We are with fraternal regard, W. Master,

"Your obedient Servants and Brothers,

"William H. White, no "Edw. Harper,'

"Lodge No. 341, Devizes."

"lacock Abbey, *December 19th,* 1825. "Sir and Brother,

"His Royal Highness our Most Worshipful Grand Master having appointed me P.G.M. of this Province, and'which I believe was duly notified to you, I will be obliged to you at your early convenience, if your lodge still meets, to send me a return with the names of all the members of your lodge, marking their offices in the lodge and their degrees in Masonry, as also their residences and profession, likewise the day of meeting of the lodge. "I am, Sir and Brother,

"Yours fraternally,

"J. R. Grosett. "TotheW.M., 341."

Some few years after the appointment of Brother J. E. Grosett dissatisfaction appears to have been felt at the few meetings of the Provincial Grand Lodge, and the want of personal interest in Masonry and the brethren shown by the P.G.M., owing to his ill-health and absence abroad. This feeling was expressed in the *Freemasons' Quarterly Review* for 1835, p. 209, as follows:—

"Several brethren of Wiltshire have drawn our attention to the continued indisposition and necessary absence abroad of the1 R. W. Prov. G.M. Brother Grosett, in consequence of which no Provincial Grand Lodge has been held for six years!! This Province was, till this unfortunate visitation of Providence, one of the most zealous and active in the craft: apathy has succeeded. In all societies the ruling authorities should remember how much their example determines the character of those over whom they preside. If the chief be active and courteous, the subordinates will be emulous and persevering. We earnestly but respectfully call the attention of the Deputy Grand Master of the Province of Wilts, whose private character has endeared him to all hearts, not to permit any longer delay, but to summon his brethren; they await but that summons to evince their former zeal, and prove that although the Tyler's sword has been long in the scabbard, it may yet gleam in the sunshine."

Though a copy of the above was sent to the D.P.G.M. as expressive of the feelings of the brethren, no official notice appears to have been taken of the matter, nor further steps on the part of the brethren, until upon the Lodge of Eectitude sending a memorial in 1841 to the D.P.G.M. conveying the wish of the lodge that a Provincial Grand Lodge should be held during the summer at Chippenham, and a reply having been received stating his inability to hold a Provincial Grand Lodge during 1841 on account of his ill-health, it was resolved that a respectful communication be sent to the "Prov. G.M. Bro. Grosett, showing the deplorable state of Freemasonry in the Province of Wilts, and asking his hind aid and assistance towards its revival."

We hear no more of this subject until 1852, when resolutions were passed by the lodges at Mohkton Parleigh and Swindon, that it was desirable that the office of Provincial Grand Master should be renewed; and in February, 1853, a formal petition by the Swindon Lodge to the Grand Master to appoint a Provincial Grand Master was signed in open lodge, resulting in the happy announcement two months afterwards that the office had been offered to, and accepted by, Lord Methuen, who was subsequently installed with great ceremony at Swindon on the 6th of September, 1853, by Sir W. W. Wynn, Bart., M.P., the Provincial Grand Master for North Wales, in the presence of a large number of distinguished Masons, when the following patent was read in open lodge:— PATENT.

Zetland, G. M.

To all and every our Right Worshipful, Worshipful, and Loving Brethren. *We,* Thomas Dundas, Earl of Zetland, Baron Dundas of Aike, in the county of York, Grand Master of the most Ancient and Honourable Fraternity of Free and Accepted Masons of England,

Send Greeting.

Know ye that we of the great trust and confidence reposed in our right trusty and well-beloved Brother the Right Honourable Frederick Henry Paul Methuen, Baron Methuen of Corsham, in the county of Wilts, &c, &c, &c, bo hereby constitute and appoint him JJroointial (Srsnb faster for the said

County of Wilts, with full power and authority to make Masons, and constitute and regulate Lodges, as occasion may require,—subject nevertheless to our approval. And Also to do and execute all and every such other acts and things appertaining to the said office, as usually have been or ought to be done and executed by other Provincial Grand Masters. He, the Right Honourable Frederick Henry Paul Methuen, Baron Methuen, taking special care that all and every the Members of every Lodge he shall constitute have been regularly made Masons, and that they and the members of all other Lodges within his Province do observe, perform, and keep all and every the Rules, Orders, and Regulations, contained in the Book of Constitutions, except such as have been or may be repealed at any Quarterly Communication or other General Meeting; together also 'with all such Rules, Orders, Regulations, and Instructions, as shall from time to time be transmitted by us, or by the Right Honourable Charles AnderSon Worsley Pelham, Earl Of Yarborough, Baron Yarborough, Baron Ausley, &c, &c, &c, our *Deputy Grand Master,* or by any of our successors, Grand Masters, or their Deputies for the time being. And We do will and require you, the said Provincial Grand Master, to cause at least one General Meeting or Communication to be held in *every year,* and that you promote on these and all other occasions whatever may be for the honour and advantage of Masonry, and the benefit of the Grand Charity. Jlnb that you yearly send to us or our successors, Grand Masters, an account in writing of the proceedings therein, and also do forthwith transmit to us a particular statement of what Lodges you constitute, and when and where holden, with a List of the several Members of the said Lodges, and copies of all such Rules, Orders, and

Regulations as shall be made for the good government of the same, with whatever else you shall do by virtue of these presents. And that at the same time you remit to the Treasurer of the Society for the time being, at London,

jive guinea) sterling for every Lodge you shall constitute, for the use of the Grand Lodge and other necessary purposes.

Given at London, under our Hand and Seal of Masonry, this 2nd day of March, A.L. 5853, A.D. 1853.

By command of the M.W. Grand Master, W. H. White, G.S. Yarborough, D.G.M.

From the date of the appointment of Lord Methuen as Provincial Grand Master, Masonry took deep root in this county, and has continued ever since to flourish and increase; for at the end of the same year the Lansdowne Lodge of Unity was renovated at Chippenham, the next year the Trowbridge Lodge was revived, at the beginning of 1856 the lodge at Devizes was reinstituted, and since then lodges have been constituted at Bradf ordon-Avon, New Swindon, Warminster, and Marlborough, and the number of brethren of the Province has been steadily increasing.

The year 1871 closed in with a deep feeling of anxiety pervading the whole country on account of the grievous and well-nigh fatal illness of the Grand Master of our Order, H.E.H. the Prince of Wales; but when, after weeks of anxiety felt by the whole nation, it pleased the c

Most High, to restore his Royal Highness to health, then foremost among all who expressed their thankfulness were the Freemasons of England.

A special Provincial Grand Lodge of Emergency was convened on the 20th of March, 1872, when the following Addresses, which had been previously agreed upon, and were splendidly illuminated on vellum, were signed by the P.G.M. on behalf of the Province:—

"To The Queen's Most Excellent Majesty.

"May it please your Majesty,

"We, the Ancient, Free, and Accepted Masons of the Province of Wilts, in Provincial Grand Lodge assembled, hereby desire to offer to your Majesty our most sincere and heartfelt congratulations upon the recovery of his Royal Highness the Prince of Wales from his late protracted and dangerous illness.

We fervently pray that it may please the Most High to restore his ftoyal Highness completely and speedily to his former health, and that he may long continue to enjoy the same. We also earnestly hope that Almighty God may be pleased to bless your Majesty with health and strength to reigrt many years over a happy and contented people, among whom none are to be found more loyal and affectionately attached to your Majesty and royal house than the Freemasons of this

Province. i

"We remain,

"With the profoundest veneration, Madam,

"Your Majesty's most faithful subjects and dutiful Servants,

"Methuen, P.G.M., "On behalf of the Province.

"Chippenham, 20th March, 1872."

"To ms Royal Highness The Prince Of Wales. "May it please your Royal Highness,

"We, the Wiltshire Provincial Grand Lodge of Ancient, Free, and Accepted Masons beg to offer you our grateful and heartfelt congratulations upon your recovery from your recent severe and dangerous illness.

We earnestly pray the great Architect of the Universe that He may be pleased speedily to re-establish your Royal Highness in the full enjoyment of your former health, and also that you may be spared for many years to live amongst us, and ever find that your brethren in Masonry are firmly and affectionately attached to your Royal Highness.

"We remain, "With the greatest respect,

"Sir,

"Your Royal Highness's most dutiful and fraternally devoted Servants,

"methuen, P.G.M., "On behalf of the Province. "Chippenham, 20th March, 1872."

The following gracious replies to the foregoing Addresses were afterwards received:—

"whitehall, *July 2nd,* 1872. "Sir,

"I have had the honour to lay before the Queen the loyal and dutiful Address of the Provincial Grand Lodge of Freemasons of Wiltshire, on the occasion of the illness of his Royal Highness the Prince of Wales.

"I have to inform you that her Majesty was pleased to receive the Address very graciously.

"I am, Sir,

"Your obedient Servant,

"H. A. Bruce. "Henry C. Tombs, Esq. , "Wootton Bassett."

"Marlborough House, "pall Mall, S. W., *"June 18th,* 1872. "General Sir William Knollys presents his compliments to Lord Methuen, and is desired by the Prince of Wales to acknowledge the receipt of an Address from the Wiltshire Provincial Grand Lodge of Ancient, Free, and Accepted Masons, and to convey his Royal Highness's sincere thanks for their kind congratulations on his recovery. "The Right Honourable Lord Methuen."

We next come to a far brighter scene; for among the pleasant days in Wiltshire Masonry the 22nd of November, 1876, will ever hold a place, on account of the presence at Provincial Grand Lodge of our E.W. Brother, his Eoyal Highness Prince Leopold, P.G.M. for Oxfordshire; and the presentation to the E. W. Provincial Grand Master, Lord Methuen, of a standard bearing his arms, with supporters and motto, and the name of the Province, as a token of the high esteem and regard entertained for him by the brethren of the Province, and as an expression of their gratitude for the efficient and zealous manner in which his lordship had presided over Masonic affairs in Wiltshire for so many years. The occasion, too, was noteworthy on account of the large assemblage of distinguished Masons, belonging to our own and several other Provinces.

The Provincial Grand Lodge was held at Warminster for the first time, the brethren assembling soon after mid-day in the Town Hall. His Eoyal Highness, on his arrival, was conducted by the V. W. the Deputy

Provincial Grand Master (Brother Gabriel Goldney, M.P.), to the rohingroom, where the Prince was received by the Provincial Grand Master and his officers, who subsequently formed a procession to the lodgeroom, where the brethren received them with the usual honours.

After the Provincial Grand Lodge had been opened in ample form, the Provincial Grand Secretary, Brother Henry C. Tombs, called the roll of the lodges, and also read the minutes of the Provincial Grand Lodge, held at Chippenham on the 5th of November, 1875, which were confirmed and signed.

The Provincial Grand Master then rose and said that before proceeding further with the business of the lodge, it was his pleasing duty, on their behalf and his own, to express the great pleasure and gratification they felt at the presence of their illustrious visitor, his Eoyal Highness Prince Leopold. The attendance of the Prince spoke well for the progress of the craft in this Province, as it showed that the conduct and management of the lodges in this Province had, as far as his Eoyal Highness's knowledge of them was concerned, met with his approval, and it was a great encouragement to the Masons of Wiltshire, and an inducement to others to enter the order. He earnestly hoped that his Eoyal Highness would never have reason to regret, but rather that he would ever have cause to feel proud, that he belonged to a Wiltshire Masonic Lodge. (Loud cheers.)

The brethren then rose and saluted the Prince with the honours due to his exalted rank.

The Deputy Grand Master, with several of the Grand Officers, then retired, and shortly afterwards returned in procession, with a very handsome standard, bearing the arms, supporters, and motto of the Provincial Grand Master. The procession having halted in the centre of the lodge,

The Deputy Grand Master (Brother G. Goldney, M.P.), amidst much cheering, said he stood before them as the mouthpiece of the Provincial Grand Lodge, and of all the lodges in the Wiltshire Province, to express to the Provincial Grand Master the great esteem and regard which they all entertained, and had for a long time entertained, for him, and also to express the gratitude they felt towards him for the able way in which he had conducted Masonry in Wiltshire for a great many years,—in number almost approaching a generation of man. (Cheers.) During the time that Lord Methuen had presided over the Province several new lodges had been consecrated, the older lodges had been increased in numbers, and there could be no doubt that a great amount of the success of Masonry in this Province was largely due to the able supervision of their Provincial Grand Master. (Cheers.) What he uttered in words now, would, he was sure, be heartily responded to by all present; but his words would pass away, and it was with the view of perpetuating, as far as they could, the memory of the benefits the Province had received under Lord Methuen's presidency, that they now asked his lordship's acceptance of the standard bearing the arms of his family, hoping that the business of the Provincial Grand Lodge of Wiltshire might long be carried on under the guidance of his lordship. (Loud and prolonged cheers.)

The standard was then fixed above the Provincial Grand Master's seat, amidst the applause of the brethren.

The Provincial Grand Master (who was greeted with loud cheers on rising) assured the brethren that he felt great difficulty in sufficiently expressing the high and deep sense he entertained of the presentation of this standard to the Provincial Grand Lodge. The difficulty was that he hardly knew how to portion out to himself any credit for the success of Masonry in this Province. That success was not, and had not been, owing so much—as his excellent brother, the Deputy Provincial Grand Master, had been kind enough to say —to his exertions, hut was attributable in the main to the exertions of others who had acted for him, to those who, being at the head of the different lodges in the Province, had so successfully brought those lodges to their present influential position, to the brethren throughout the Province, and to the hearty exertions of all to promote the good and the benefit

of the craft. (Cheers.) He begged to express his very strongest feelings of gratitude for the honour they had done him on that occasion. (Cheers.) At this, as at all other times when he had appeared before them, there had never been expressed towards him anything but the greatest kindness and courtesy. (Cheers.) He assured them that so long as he should have the honour of presiding over this Province he should look with f eelings of pride at the banner which they had just been kind enough to present to him. (Loud cheers.)

The Provincial Grand Master then presented charity jewel bars to Brother Stokes, P.G.S.W., and Brother Henry C. Tombs, P.G.S. Referring to the former, the P.G.M. said he had performed his duties in a manner that had given great satisfaction; and, addressing the latter, his lordship said the same remarks applied to Brother Tombs, who was entitled to their warmest thanks for the assiduity and attention he had always shown in promoting the interests of the craft. (Cheers.) It gave him much pleasure to hand Brother Tombs this additional token of his services to Masonry, and he was sure there was no brother who deserved it more than did Brother Tombs. (Loud cheers.)

The P.G.M. appointed and invested the Provincial Grand Officers as follows:—Henry C. Tombs, 355, P.G.S.W. and P.G.S.; Frederick Hastings Goldney, W.M., 626, P.GJ.W.; E. Gardiner, 335, P.G.C.; Eichard Bradford, 355, P. G.T.; H. Blackmore, 586, P.G.E.; John V. Toone, 1478, P.S.G.D.; John Chandler, 355, P.G. Director of Ceremonies; Col. J. F. Everett, 1478, P.G. Assistant Director of Ceremonies; Col. J. E. Magrath, 1271, P.G.8.B.; W. S. Stodart, 586, P.G. Poursuivant; Walter Hume Long, 626, P.G.A.P.; J. Savory, P.G. Tyler.

The P.G.M. again rose and said that in addressing a few words to the members of the Provincial Grand Lodge, it was unnecessary for him to add to the observations he had already made in reference to the progress of Masonry in this Province,.and the excellent management of the respective lodges, ex-

cept to say this, that, there was one brother present to whom the success of Masonry in this Province was more due than to any one else, and he need scarcely mention that he alluded to their worthy and esteemed brother, Sir Daniel Gooch. (Cheers.) It would ill become him, holding the position he did, and having been so greatly honoured by the brethren of the Province, if he did not acknowledge that it was owing to Sir Daniel's exertions, when holding the office of Deputy Provincial Grand Master, that Masonry had taken such firm root in this Province. (Cheers.) They must all deeply regret that they had lost Sir Daniel Gooch as their Deputy Provincial Grand Master, but he had become Provincial Grand Master for Berks and Bucks, and he (the P.G.M.) felt sure that the brethren of Wiltshire would heartily join him in wishing Sir Daniel all possible health and success in carrying out that important office. (Hear, hear.) Now it only remained for him to thank the brethren, which he did most heartily, for their attendance to-day, and for the exertions that one and all had made to further the interests of the craft; and also to thank them again most sincerely for the honour they had done him, and the compliment they had paid him. He trusted that Masonry would nourish in the future even more than it had done in the past, and that those with whom he was associated would be able to feel that through their exertions a sound fabric of Masonry had been raised in this Province. (Cheers.)

The business of the Province was then proceeded with, and Grand Lodge was subsequently closed in ample form.

The brethren afterwards sat down to a banquet, at which the E.W. the P.G. M. presided, and the company included—H.E.H. Prince Leopold, P.G.M. for Oxfordshire; Gabriel Goldney, M.P., D. P.G.M. Wilts; Et. Hon. Lord Henry Thynne, M.P., P.G. Supt. Wilts; SirW. W.Wynn, Bart., P.G.M. North Wales; Sir Daniel Gooch, Bart., M.P., P.G.M. Berks and Bucks; W. H. Poynder (High Sheriff), 626; Arthur E. Guest, P.P.GS. W. Dorset; Henry C. Tombs, P.S.G.W. , P.G. Sec.; Col. the Hon. Percy Fielding, 1478; F. H. Goldney, W.M. 626, P.J.G.W.; V. F. Benett Stanford, M.P., 1478; E. H. CoUins, 357 and 1478; H. Merrick, W.M. 1271; Henry A. Fane, 472; Capt. Bradford, P.G.T. Wilts; A. MitcheU, P.M. 335; T. Lord, P.M. 335, P.Z., P.P.G.S.D. Wilts; J. V. Toone, W. M. 1478; E. Elling, 1478; J. Hammond, S.W. 1533; T. Bush, PPG. Chaplain; C. Milsom, P.PG.S.D. Wilts; Eev. T. F. Eavenshaw, P.G. Chap. Eng., P.P.G.W. Wilts; E. Cook, P.P.G.S.B. Wilts; John Chandler, P.P.G.8.W. Wilts; S. J. Haden, Sec. 1478; J. K. Harris, 1478; S. E. Jefferys, 1478; Wm. Martin, 1478; T. Marshman, 1478; John Smith, 1478; H. E. Vincent, 1478; G. Pike, Steward, 1478; A. Tucker, Secretary, 586; H. Hardick, Treasurer, 1478; C. Price, Steward, 1478; J. W. Titt, I.G. 1478; G. H. Bush, 1478; W. Pullin, jun., 1478; S. Gauntlett, P.M. 632, P.P.G.S.B.; T. Ponting, S.W. 1478; J. Eeeves, 1478; T. Eeeves, 1478;-S. Cross, 1478; J. Coombs, 1478; G. J. Cosburn, Secretary, 574; and many others.

Grace having been said, and the usual loyal toasts proposed,

The E.W. the Provincial Grand Master rose amidst cheering, and said he felt it difficult to perform the task that now devolved upon him, pleasant and honourable as it was. He regretted that he was not gifted with that eloquence which might have done proper justice to the toast which stood next on the list, and he was also aware that a certain amount of delicacy stared him in the face, and prevented his expressing his feelings fully with regard to the illustrious Prince whose health he was about to propose. (Loud cheers.) The Prince's modesty was only equalled by his worth, and he (Lord Methuen) was aware that his Eoyal Highness would be by no means gratified by any elaborate expression of the opinions they entertained respecting him. He would content himself by congratulating this Province upon the presence at their lodge of such an illustrious brother as Prince Leopold. (Cheers.) He could safely say that so long as it might please his Eoyal Highness to dwell in the Province of Wilts, he would find none

more loyal to his illustrious house, and none more kindly disposed towards himself than the Masons of Wiltshire. (Cheers.) The toast having been drunk with full honours, His Eoyal Highness Prince Leopold, rising, was greeted with great applause, and replied in the following terms:—" Eight Worshipful Sir and Brethren,—I rise to return my most sincere thanks for the cordial terms in which the Provincial Grand Master has proposed my health, and also to return thanks to all the brethren for the kind reception they have given to this toast. (Cheers.) Although I have spent little more than a few weeks in Wiltshire, this is already the second occasion on which I have received a hearty reception from the brethren of this Province. (Cheers.) I can assure you that this fact in no small degree increases my appreciation of this county, and of this neighbourhood in particular. (Loud cheers.) It seems to me that wherever a Mason may take up his residence, and however much he may previously have been a stranger in the county, he is sure to find there a nucleus of ready-made friends. (Loud cheers.) And this, brethren, is an advantage which, I am sure you will agree, cannot be valued too highly. (Loud cheers.) I must add that it is a special pleasure to me to make the acquaintance of my brother Masons in Wiltshire, and to find my highly valued friend, Lord Methuen, in charge of the Province. (Cheers.) Although there are probably many present who have enjoyed the Provincial Grand Master's friendship a greater number of years than I have, I can at least say that I have known him as long almost as I have known any one, and I need not add that to know him is to appreciate a manly, straightforward, and thoroughly English character. (Loud cheers.) Inviting you to drink 'The health of the Provincial Grand Master,' I congratulate you upon having so genial and cheery a chief, and I ask you to join me in praying that he may be spared for many, many years to preside over this Province." (Loud cheers.)

The toast having been received with the customary honours, the Prince him-

self leading the "firing" peculiar to the craft,

The Provincial Grand Master said he should indeed be wanting in the commonest feelings of gratitude if he did not respond to the toast so kindly brought forward by his Eoyal Highness, although the compliment was so very undeserved. (Cries of " No, no.") Whatever merits or demerits he might possess, he must confess that the progress of Masonry in this Province was not so much owing to him, as his Eoyal Highness had been kind enough to intimate, as to the labours of others; and he felt how unworthy he was of the honour that had been conferred upon him. (Cries of "No, no.") Still, however unworthy he might be of the Prince's too flattering remarks, he was not unmindful of the kindness and generosity of the brethren who had so cordially received the toast. (Loud cheers.)

The healths of the Deputy Provincial Grand Master, of the High Sheriff, of Sir Watkin Wynn, of Sir Daniel Gooch, were subsequently drunk, together with usual Masonic toasts, and thus concluded an eventful day in the Masonic history of the County.

The next occasion of great interest was upon the completion of the first quarter of a century of the rule of the Provincial Grand Master, Lord Methuen, when the brethren, to mark their high appreciation of the manner in which his lordship had conducted the business of the Province during his long tenure of office, and the benefits conferred by him upon the cause of Masonry, subscribed for the purchase of a pair of magnificent silver candelabra, and presented them, together with an illuminated address, at the Provincial Grand Lodge held at the Town Hall, Swindon, on the 8th of November, 1878.

The Provincial Grand Lodge met at two o'clock, when there were present: — Brothers Eight Hon. the Lord Methuen, P.G.M. Wilts; Gabriel Goldney, M.P., V.W.D., P.G.M. Wilts; Sir Daniel Gooch, Bart., M.P., P.G.M. Berks and Bucks; Eight Hon. Lord H. T. Thynne, M.P., P.G. Supt. Wilts; J. Case,

P.G.D. Eng.; Col. Basevi, Gloucester; W. H. Poynder; Walter Long, W.M. 632; Henry C. Tombs, P.G.D. Eng.,. P. P.S.G.W., and P.G. Sec. Wilts; F. H. Goldney, Past G. Steward, Eng., P.P.J. G.W. and P.G. Treas. Wilts; E. Trinder, P.G. Sec. Gloucester; Genl. H,, Doherty, 33, P.P.S.C.W. Somerset, P.P.S.G. D. Wilts Henry Calley, W.M. 1533; Henry Kinneir, P.P.S.G.W. John Chandler, P.P.S.G.W. and P.G. Dir. Cer. Wilts G. L. Lopes; J. Campbell Maclean, W.M. of No. 355 the Eeceiving Lodge; E. N. Fowler, P.G. Purs. Wilts A. L. Goddard, 355; Col. Everett, 1478; Thos. Graham P.P.J.G.W.; Eichard Bradford, P.P.S.G.W.; Eob Stokes, P.P. S.G.W.; W. F. Gooch, P.P.S.G.W.; T. H Chandler, P.P.S.G.W.; John Toomer, P. P.J.G.W. Arthur Law, P.G. Chap.; W. Nott, P.P.J.G.W. Charity Organization Society; J. H. Calley, E. J. Sewell, CotswoldLodge; E. deM. Lawson, P.P. S.G.W. J. W. Whatley, P.P.J.G.D.; T. Young, Past G Steward, Eng.; Wm. Affleck, P.M. 355; F. H. Phillips, W.M. 626; Geo. Pike, W.M. 1478; F. Gardner, W.M 335; E. T. Payne, P.G.D. Eng., P.P.S.G.W. Wilts; and many other brethren.

After the Provincial Grand Lodge had been opened in ample form, Brother Henry C. Tombs, P.G.D., Prov. G.S., read the minutes, which were put to the meeting and approved. He also read the following letter:—

"Darmstadt, 21th October, 1878.

"Dear Sir and Brother,

"H.E.H. Prince Leopold desires me to express the regret he feels at not being able to be present at the forthcoming Prov. Grand Lodge at Swindon. It would have been especially gratifying to H.E.H. to be present, when your P.G. Master, an old and trusted friend of our Koyal Family, receives the honourable recognition that he has so well earned from the brethren.

"Perhaps you will kindly be an interpreter to the P.G.M. of his Eoyal Highness's feelings.

"Faithfully and fraternally yours,

"E. H. Collins.

"Hnry C. Tombs, Esq., Prov. Grand Sec, &c."

And letters were read from Brothers S. Watson Taylor, John Hervey, G.S., and other distinguished Masons.

Brother P. H. Goldney, Provincial Grand Treasurer, presented the report and accounts of the Province, which were very satisfactory, showing a balance in hand of £31 8s. as against £14 for last year. There was also a balance of £57 12s. 6d. to the credit of the Charity Pund, out of which the Charity Committee had come to the conclusion that it was desirable that the Province should vote fifty guineas to the Eoyal Masonic Benevolent Institution, to endow the chair of the Provincial Grand Master with a Vice-Presidentship of that institution.

Brother Gabriel Goldney, M.P., Deputy Provincial Grand Master, then rose and said—The brethren were about to perform a duty that he was quite satisfied would meet with the approbation of all present. They were there with closed windows and borrowed lights, with all the mysteries of their craft, and the insignia of their Order; but they were about to perform an act which he was sure would be in sympathy and harmony with the feelings of the outside world, who, he believed, if they had it in their power, would appreciate the object in view and the means taken to carry it out quite as much as the brethren there assembled. The brethren were about to show their lasting testimony of feelings of esteem, regard, admiration, and gratitude for the services which had been rendered to them by their Eight Worshipful Provincial Grand Master. He would ask Brother Tombs to request the Committee and the Grand Deacons to introduce into Grand Lodge a testimonial which they would heartily, respectfully, and with every feeling of kindness and love, wish to offer to the Provincial Grand Master.

The brethren named then retired and returned in a few minutes, bearing two massive silver candelabra and a handsome illuminated address on vellum, and placed them on the table in the centre of the lodge.

The Deputy Provincial Grand Master, addressing the Provincial Grand Master, said that he was deputed, on behalf of the Freemasons of the Province of Wiltshire, to offer to his lordship the testimonial now before him in recognition of the feelings which they entertained with respect to the good his lordship had done, not only for Masonry in the Province of Wiltshire, but for Masonry in general, by the manner in which he had acted as their Provincial Grand Master for the last five-and-twenty years. He knew of nothing which they could give that would adequately represent the brethren's feelings for his lordship's kindness, but as Masons they could offer their respectful thanks to him for what he had done. The testimonial, however, which they now presented would show to others who came after them the value the brethren set on his lordship's presidency over them. The candelabra and address, now in lodge, the brethren asked his lordship's acceptance of. He was sure that no man had ever earned greater feelings of respect and kindly sentiment from those amongst whom he lived, than had his lordship in his position of a country gentleman and as Provincial Grand Master. His acts of friendship, his genial and courteous manner, and his liberality of feeling, as well as of action, were acknowledged by every one who came in contact with him, either socially or officially. He trusted that his lordship's life might be long spared, and that they might for many years have the advantage of seeing him preside in that chair, and the brethren knew perfectly well that so long as he did so Masonry would flourish in the Province. The brethren had already heard from the Treasurer's report the great increase which had taken place in the Freemasonry of the Province; how the numbers of the brethren had gradually increased from 300 to 350, and then again from 350 to 450, and he doubted not that in future years a similar state of progress would be witnessed. The charitable funds of the Province had likewise increased, and they had been able to dispense those funds in a praiseworthy manner. He believed that the increase in the number of Freemasons of the Province, and the increase in the charitable funds, were mainly due to the interest which his lordship always took in

D these matters, to his own personal dignity, to his wellknown character, and to the kindness, firmness, and forbearance ever displayed by him to the brethren, more especially when in the chair of Provincial Grand Lodge. Masonry had now attained to such an elevated position as to encourage people in the principles it professed. His lordship had assisted in raising it to this high position in the lodges of the country, and he trusted, as he had said before, that Masonry in that Province would long have the advantage of his presidency over it.

Lord Methuen, in reply, said— "Brethren, I rise, I assure you, with very great difficulty to express to you but a very small amount of that deep gratitude I feel to you all for the very kind appreciation you have shown of my humble efforts in favour of Masonry, which you have shown towards me this day. If I but inadequately express my feelings you must not attribute it to a want of gratitude on my part, but to a want of power to express myself as I would wish to all of you this day. When I behold those magnificent candelabra, and consider not only their pecuniary value, but their artistic quality, when I see that beautiful testimonial which you have presented to me, I cannot help saying to myself, What is it that I have done to render myself worthy of so much kindness on the part of the Freemasons of Wiltshire? I cannot but say that although I may to some little extent have benefited the craft during the time that I have had the honour to preside over this Province, I am sure that the amount of generosity and kindly feeling that has been evinced towards me this day is as multiplied by it ten or even a hundredfold. It is more than anything I had to expect of you. For many generations I trust those splendid specimens of your generosity and kindness will go down to those who, I hope and trust, will have the same feeling towards the Masons of this Province that I have myself, which is, and always has been, one of the kind-

est and most heartfelt sympathy for all of you. It would not do for me to detain you longer by any further observations on what is to me the happiest and, I can assure you, the very proudest moment of my connection with Masonry, not only because this testimonial comes from the brethren belonging to the Province over which I have the honour to preside, but also because those brethren belong to that county in which so many of those of my family who have gone before me have lived. It is, I assure you, a double gratification to me to know that that splendid testimonial is one which sprang from the hearts of Masons. I tender you all my best and sincerest thanks for the great honour that you have done me, and for the liberality, generosity, and kindly feelings you have evinced for me. I trust that for many years I may continue to have the pleasure of presiding over the interests of Masonry in this Province."

Brother Henry 0. Tombs, Provincial Grand Secretary, then read the address as follows:—

"To The Right Honourable The Lord Methuen, Right Worshipful Provincial Grand Master Of Wiltshire.

"Right Worshipful Sir,

"We, the Ancient, Free, and Accepted Masons of the Province of Wiltshire, respectfully desire to tender to you our affectionate and fraternal congratulations on the completion of the twenty-fifth year of your high office as Grand Master of this Province, and at the same time to beg your acceptance of the accompanying

Pair Of Silver Candelabra, which we offer as a small proof of our great appreciation of the unfailing interest and beneficial influence which you have displayed in the active government of this Province for a quarter of a century, and of our esteem and regard for you personally.

"We fervently pray the G.A.O.T.TJ. that you may for many years be blessed with health and strength to continue your kind and impartial rule, and that you will find all future Wiltshire Masons to be imbued with the same loyalty and devotion towards yourself as those

who have now the privilege of subscribing themselves, with every feeling of respect,

"Your fraternally grateful, faithful, and obedient Servants, "Signed on behalf of the Province,

"gabl. Goldney,.m.p., V.W.D.P.G.M. Wilts. "Provincial Grand Lodge, Swindon, 8th November, 1878."

Provincial Grand Lodge.

Thos. Hicks Chandler, P.S.G.W.

William Nott, P. J.G.W.

Frederick Hastings Goldney, P.G. Steward, Eng., P.P.J.G.W., P.G. Treasurer.

Henry C. Tombs, P.G.D. Eng., P.P.S.G. W., P.G. Secretary.

John Chandler, P.P.S.G.W., P.G. Dir. Cer.

Provincial Grand Chapter.

The Right Honourable Lord H. T. Thynne, M.P., P.G.W. Eng., P.G.N. Eng. Prov. Grand Superintendent.

Lodge of Rectitude, No. 335, Corsham. Fredk. D. Gardner, W.M.; Alfred Fudge, S.W.; Josh. Martin, J.W. *Royal Sussex Lodge of Emulation, No. 355, Swindon.* J. Campbell Maclean, W.M. ; W. Jenkins, S.W.; E. J. Hollings, J. W. *Lodge Elias de Derham, No. 586, Salisbury.* Thos. Norwood, W.M.; Ambrose Tucker, S.W.; Chas. H. Card, J. W. *Lansdowne Lodge of Unity, No. 626, Chippenham.* Fras. H. Phillips, W.M.; G. J. Bailey, S.W.; R. Careless, J.W. *Lodge of Concord, No. 632, Trowbridge.* Walter H. Long, "W.M.; Alf. R. Brown, S.W.; Thos. R. Lavington, J.W. *Lodge of Fidelity, No. 663, Devizes.* J. W. Burman, W.M.; T. H. Chandler, S.W.; Harry Howse, J.W. *Lodge of Friendship and Unity, No. 1271, Bradford-on-Avon.* Wm. E. Taylor, W.M.; George Rose, S.W.; Henry Simson, J. W. *Gooch Lodge, No. 1295, New Swindon.* Wm. H. Ludgate,W.M.; Fred. C. Kent, S.W.; Thos. Turner, J.W. *Longleat Lodge, No. 1478, Warminster.* George Pike, W.M.; J. F. Everett, S.W.; W. S. Cross, J.W. *Lodge of Loyalty, No. 1533, Marlborough.* Henry Calley, W. M.; James Carter, S.W.; Thos. Harrison, J.W.

Brother Frederick Hastings Goldney, the Provincial Grand Treasurer, afterwards stated that he had prepared a history of Freemasonry in Wiltshire, which he begged to present to the Provincial Grand Master, but at the same time regretted that, as the records of Freemasonry in the County were few and scattered before the time that his lordship undertook the government of the Province, the work was far from perfect. The manuscript was then presented to the Provincial Grand Master.

Lord Methuen said the thanks of the brethren were due to their excellent Treasurer, Brother F. H. Goldney, for his attention to the interests of Masonry, and his devoting so much time and trouble to the compilation of the work just placed in his hands; and he had no doubt that there would be few Masons in the Province who would not be glad to avail themselves of the opportunity afforded by such a valuable work to learn more about the Freemasonry of the County in bygone years. He therefore asked that it might be printed for distribution among the Brethren.

Brother Sir Daniel Gooeh added a few complimentary remarks to the same effect, and seconded the request that the work should be printed.

Lord Methuen then declared all the offices in Provincial Grand Lodge vacant, and appointed the following brethren Provincial Grand Officers for the ensuing year:—

John Toomer, 355 Prov. S.G.W.

General H. E. Doherty, 335... Prov. J. G.W.

H. Crockett, 1478 Prov. G. Chap.

Frederick Hastings Goldney, 626. Prov. G. Treas.

W. Nott, 663 Prov. G. Keg.

Henry C. Tombs, 355 Prov. G. Sec.

J. Campbell Maclean, 355... Prov. S. G.D.

Walter H. Long, 632 Prov. J.G.D.

W. J. Mann, 632 Prov. G.S. of W.

John Chandler, 355 Prov. G.D. of C.

F. H. Phillips Prov. G.A.D. of C.

T. E. Liddiard, 355 Prov. G. Swd. B.

G. Whitehead, 355 Prov. G. Org.

F. Baldwin, 355 Prov. G. Purst.

W. Affleck, 355 Prov. G.A. Purst.

W. Futcher, 386 Prov. G. Std. B.

John Savory, 355 Prov. G. Tyler.

Lord Methuen afterwards stated that from the numerous reports received from the lodges in the Province, the position of Wiltshire Freemasonry was very satisfactory. It appeared that the members of the craft had increased in number, and that there was an increase in the subscriptions to the different charities of the Order. All this was a matter of gratification to him. The Treasurer's report showed that there was a considerable amount of money in hand, and this was highly satisfactory to the Provincial Grand Lodge. He was glad to hear from the Provincial Grand Secretary that some steps were about to be taken relative to the Boys' and Girls' Schools, so as to prevent the election of several children belonging to the same family, when there were so many children equally deserving thereby prevented from gaining admission. He must mention another subject. When they met last year there was a fear that the country might be involved in war. He was happy to say that we had escaped that calamity, and he hoped that by the blessing of God we might long be spared that most dreadful alternative of arms. He had to thank all the officers and brethren of the Province who had attended to do him honour on this occasion. He had no doubt that the interests of Masonry would be considerably furthered and increased by the interchange of those little courtesies which passed between the lodges of this Province and the lodges of other Provinces.

The office of Eegistrar has of late years become as important as its name indicates; for the Provincial Grand Eegistrar, in an annual report recorded in a register-book kept for that purpose, refers to all public matters affecting the Province, and the lodges composing it, and appends thereto tables analyzing the returns of the several lodges, showing with regard to each the number of meetings held, the number of candidates installed, the number of joining brethren, and the receipts and disbursements under various heads.

These tables show the satisfactory progress that is made year by year in Masonry in this Province, and the in-

crease in the numbers of the lodges and of the brethren.

In 1872 there were 8 Lodges and 314 members.

The Provincial Charity Organization Committee was first instituted at the Provincial Grand Lodge held on the 20th of November, 1872. It consists of the P.G. Master, the Deputy P.G. Master, the P.G. Treasurer, the P.G. Eegistrar, the P.G. Secretary, and a member from each lodge of the Province elected annually by such lodge. Its principal object is "To regulate the support to be given to candidates for the several charities of the Order, with a view to prevent the waste of strength which has for many years occurred; but so as not to infringe on the rights of any lodges or brethren to apply them in their discretion."

It had been found that the votes for the Masonic charities arising from those belonging to lodges and brethren of this Province had failed in securing the results that the numbers of such votes ought to have derived, owing to their being scattered and given away without any concerted action. This was believed to be in a great degree caused by a want of some common centre where the cases of the various candidates could be thoroughly considered, and a selection made of those thought most desirable for recommendation to the support of the lodges and brethren of Wiltshire.

Such confidence has the working of the committee inspired that there are now regularly placed at its disposal not only all the votes of all the lodges in the Province, but the greater part of the votes belonging individually to the members and friends thereof.

Any case for either of the Institutions that may arise within the Province, being, after careful investigation by the committee, found worthy of support, receives the undivided assistance of the votes of this Province.

By these means, and by the aid obtained from other Provinces with similar organizations in friendly unison with Wiltshire, it has been found practicable during the last two or three years to assure the success of all candidates at either the first or second election after their adoption by the committee.

The Provincial Grand Secretary, Brother Henry C. Tombs, who was mainly instrumental in the establishment of this committee, was its first secretary, and held that office till 1876. On his resignation in November of that year Brother William Nott, who had taken great interest in the working of the committee, was appointed, and still continues to be, its secretary, and carries on the arduous duties of the. office with much satisfaction to the brethren. It is hoped that greater scope will before long be given to the committee, by their being empowered to recommend proper objects for the application of the general charity funds of the Provincial Grand Lodge, and that thus these charity funds need not be entirely devoted to the purchase of votes for the three Masonic charitable Institutions, but may be devoted towards assisting aged and distressed Freemasons and their widows and children with pecuniary relief and education at their own homes in Wiltshire.

This Province is in a highly prosperous condition at present, as evinced by there being ten lodges with 465 members on the muster-roll, figures which compare most favourably with those of other Provinces, after due allowances are made for a greater or lesser population and area.

The large average attendance at the frequent meetings held by the several lodges throughout the year, the loyalty and obedience shown towards the Provincial Grand Master, the abundant charitable subscriptions annually given by the lodges and individual Masons, the efficient working of the various committees and officers, and the active interest displayed in Masonry by the brethren, are noticeable features of this Province; added to which, the harmony prevailing, the infrequent retirement of members from the lodges, the continual accessions to the craft, and the general desire to admit such only to a participation in our mysteries and privileges as from their moral character and social position are Ukely to add to the dignity,

efficiency, and importance of Masonry, consolidate the Masonic body in the Province, and render it an object of admiration and emulation to neighbouring Provinces and the outside 'world.

The popularity and high standing of the craft in this Province of Wiltshire, so different from what it was but a few years ago, when it could boast of but two working lodges and a score of subscribing members, is, in a great measure, due to the exertions of the P.G. M., Lord Methuen, who for upwards of a quarter of a century has had the Province under his charge, and who, by his unwavering interest in the maintenance of good order and harmony in the lodges, by his courtesy towards the brethren, by his constant attendance at the meetings of Provincial Grand Lodge, and by his impartiality in the discharge of the duties devolving upon his high office, has so materially aided in increasing the numbers of the lodges and brethren, and establishing that genuine feeling of loyalty towards himself, and good-will towards one another, which is here so happily displayed.

The noble ruler has been ably supported by his officers, of whose excellent qualifications and valuable services space will not admit of mention, beyond a passing reference to the three brethren who have filled the important office of Deputy Provincial Grand Master under him. The first of these, Sir Daniel Gooch, Bart., M.P. (whose fame as a Mason is almost as widespread as his great reputation in the outer world), bore the heat and burden of the work of the Province for sixteen years from the time of his lordship's appointment, and rested not from his labours until in 1869 he was summoned to fill the higher office of Provincial Grand Master for Berks and Bucks, whither his great popularity amongst the brethren has followed him.

On his quitting this Province the Wiltshire brethren presented to him the entire regalia and clothing of a Provincial Grand Master of beautiful workmanship, accompanied by a suitable address, expressing their congratulations upon his high appointment, their regret

at his leaving the Province, the deep sense of the obligations they were under to him, and their hopes for his happy and prosperous future.

Sir Daniel Gooch had taken great interest in the formation of the Methuen Lodge, No. 914, and so attached were the members of it to its founder, that on Sir D. Gooch assuming the rule over Berks and Bucks it was arranged, with the full consent and approbation of the Provincial Grand Master and brethren of both Provinces, for that lodge to be included in the Province of Berks and Bucks, and its place of meeting was accordingly removed in 1870 to Taplow.

To make up in some degree for this loss to Wiltshire the Gooch Lodge, No. 1295, was established at New Swindon about the same time.

The succeeding Deputy Provincial Grand Master was Brother Wittey, of Devizes; but all too soon death cut short the good work to which he so earnestly devoted himself.

In 1873 the appointment of Brother Sir Gabriel Goldney, Bart., M.P., as Deputy Provincial Grand Master was received with such good-will and ready co-operation from all the officers and brethren as to strongly mark how heartily the appointment was approved of; and his continued popularity amongst them confirms their previous favourable opinion.

Eeference must also be specially made to one of the most influential brethren in the Province, Lord Henry F. Thynne, M.P., whose high social rank, genial and courteous manner on all occasions, and unremitting exertions for the benefit of Freemasonry have endeared him to all the brethren.

In 1875 he was appointed Most Excellent Superintendent of Eoyal Arch Masonry in and over the Province of Wilts. This important Order of Masonry, though worked in this County from time to time ever since its formal recognition by the United. Grand Lodge of England in 1772, made but little progress until it was so heartily taken in hand ten years ago, and has since been so carefully fostered by this distinguished Mason, who has already 3

Chapters and 73 Companions under his rule.

To his lordship is mainly due the establishment of the Longleat Lodge; and his presence at the meetings of the Provincial Grand Lodge and Provincial Grand Chapter and other Masonic gatherings is always hailed with pleasure.

Without detracting at all from the services of many a good brother who in times past has ranged under the banner of this Province, or disregarding the merits of those who are still amongst us, mention should be particularly made of the eminent services of Brother Henry C. Tombs, the Provincial Grand Secretary, who has filled that important office for the last twelve years to the great satisfaction of the Provincial Grand Master (as frequently expressed by him in public), the approbation of the brethren, and the benefit of the craft. He has also filled the office of Provincial Grand Scribe E. since the establishment of the Eoyal Arch Provincial Grand Chapter in Wiltshire, and is a Past Grand Deacon of England.

To this brother are greatly due the present thorough state of organization of the Province, the regularity with which all the business is conducted, and the good feeling prevailing among the lodges.

s

He has given much attention to the raising of subscriptions for the Masonic charities and their efficient application, and is actively interesting himself in promoting the uniformity of working in the several lodges and chapters of the Province.

Hearty thanks are due and are hereby tendered to the different lodges and chapters who have all most generously and unreservedly lent their minute-books and records for the purposes of this publication, and especially to their secretaries, who so readily afforded their assistance; and warm acknowledgments must also be made to the several brethren who have so kindly lent documents and old correspondence illustrative of the subjects here treated of, amongst whom should be particularly mentioned the E.W. Provincial Grand

Master for Berks and Bucks; the P.G. Secretary, Brother Henry 0. Tombs; Brother W. Nott, Brother J. Chandler, Brother Prideaux Saunders, Brother Stokes, Brother Whatley, Brother Gauntlett, Brother Bevir, and others.

PROVINCIAL SENIOR GRAND WARDEN—continued. 1866. 1867. 1868. 1869. 1870. 1871. 1872. 1777. 1792. 1827. 1828. 1836. 1837. 1839. 1853. 1854. 1855. 1856. 1857. 1858. 1859. 1860. 1861. 1862. 1863.
W. Read.
E. Benham.
R. Bradford.
Henry Kinneir.
George James Parfitt.
Richard de Mulinfeldt Lawson.
Robert Stokes.
1873. John Chandler.
1874. C. W. Wyndham. 1875. Rev. C. R. Davy. 1876. Henry C. Tombs. 1877. Thomas Hicks Chandler. 1878. John Toomer. 1879. Frederick Hastings Gold

PROVINCIAL JUNIOR GRAND WARDEN.
J. Edgar, Jun.
Edward Sweeper.
James Ames.
William Gould, R.N.
William Morse Crowdy.
John James Calley.
Hinton East Drake.
Robert Withers.
M. C. Rea.
E. Roberts.
T. Goddard.
Henry Weaver.
S. Dunning.
— Collings.
F. O. Hodgkinaon.
W. Biggs.
C. F. Marshall.
G. P. Stancomb.
1864. E. Benham. 1865. Richard Bradford. 1866. Rev.T.F.T. Ravenshaw. 1867. Richard de M. Lawson. 1868. Henry Kinneir. 1869. John Chandler. 1870. John Toomer. 1871. C. W. Wyndham. 1872. Horatio Ward. 1873. Edward Turner Payne. 1874. Thomas Graham. 1875. E. R. Ing. 1876. Frederick Hastings Gold ney. 1877. William Nott. 1878. General H. E. Doherty. 1879. Walter Hume Long,M.P. PROVINCIAL

GRAND TREASURER. 1777. James Wilkinson.
1827. John Harding Sheppard.
1829. „.,
1865. Samuel Wittey. 1866. „ „ 1867. „ 1868. „ „ 1869. Richard Bradford.
1870.
1871.
1872.
1873. „ ' „ 1874. 1875. 1876. 1877. Frederick Hastings Gold ney. 1878. 1879. PROVINCIAL GRAND 1854. P. W. Cother. 1855. T. Goddard. 1856. — Colling3. 1857. George Firmin. 1858. 1859. W. Biggs. 1860. „ 1861. C. F. Marshall. 1862. E. T. Payne. 1863. John Chandler. 1864. H. Calf. 1865. Richard de M. Lawson. 1866. „ „ REGISTRAR—continued. 1867. C. W. Wyndham. 1868. E. A. Moore. 1869. Robert Stokes. 1870. William C. Merriman. 1871. William Nott. 1872. Thomas Graham. 1873. John Spencer. 1874. S. H. Perman. 1875. R. D. Commans. 1876. Humphrey Blackmore. 1877. Alexander James Braid. 1878. William Nott. 1879. „ „ PROVINCIAL SENIOR GRAND DEACON—continued. 1860. C. F. Marshall. 1861. H. C. Levander. 1862. John Chandler. 1863. H. Calf. 1864. Samuel Hayward. 1865. W. Gibbs. 1866. J. Toomer. 1867. E. A. Moore.-1868. Frederick King. 1869. William Nott. 1870. F. V. Holloway. PROVINCIAL JUNIOR GRAND DEACON. 1827. — Crowdy.
1829. —Withers.
1837. Samuel Bennett.
1853. P. W. Cother. 1854. T. Pain. 1855. W. F. Gooch. 1856. Thomas Large Henly. 1857. Joseph Burt. 1858. C. W. Hind. 1859. G. P. Stancomb. 1860. Samuel Wittey. 1861. E. T-Payne. 1862. Richard Bradford. 1863. E. Benham. 1864. W. Read. 1865. E. A. Moore. PROVINCIAL GRAND SUPERINTENDENT OF WORKS. 1827. William Noble. 1829. —Drake. 1837. William Brown. 1853. Henry Weaver. 1854. E. Roberts. 1855. C. W. Hind. 1856 1857. 1871. Charles Milsom. 1872. A. J. Braid. 1873. General H. E. Doherty. 1874. Frederick Hastings Gold ney. 1875. J. A. Lush, M.P. 1876. John V. Toone. 1877. John Godwin. 1878. J.

Campbell Maclean. 1879. Henry J. Birch. 1866. S. G. Mitchell. 1867. M. McHugh. 1868. G. T. Dicks. 1869. Wakefield Simpson. 1870. H. P. Blackmore. 1871. Thomas R. Lord. 1872. Henry James Birch. 1873. Henry Joseph Guyon. 1874. Thomas Prideaux Saunders. 1875. J. L. Whatley. 1876. Henry Calley. 1877. Thomas Raymond. 1878. Walter Hume Long, M.P. 1879. Samuel Gauntlett. 1858. C. F. Marshall. 1859. 1860. Thomas Chandler. 1861. John Chandler. 1862. J. Allen. 1863. William Read. 1864. Richard de M. Lawson. 1865. PROVINCIAL GRAND SUPERINTENDENT OF WORKS —continued. 1866. C. W. Wyndham. 1867. Charles Feaviour. 1868. Wakefield Simpson. 1869. Thomas R. Lord. 1870. SirG.Goldney.Bart.M.P. 1871. John Godwin. 1872. Frederick Hastings Gold ney. 1873. Joseph Armstrong. 1874. Thomas Ponting. 1875. Francis Barnett. 1876. 1877. Samuel Gauntlett. 1878. William J. Mann. 1879. Alfred Browne. PROVINCIAL GRAND DIRECTOR OF CEREMONIES. 1827. — Withers. 1829. John Brown. 1837. ,, ,, 1853. J. W. Brown. 1854. B. Robinson. 1855. Thomas Large Henly. 1856. 1857. F. Webber. 1858. W. Biggs. 1859. Richard Bradford. I860. 1861. J. M. Cardell. 1862. Francis Stewart Wilmot. 1863. Richard de M. Lawson. 1864. J. Toomer. 1865. J. Holloway. 1866. ,, ,, 1867. W. H. Tarrant. 1868. William C. Merriman. 1869. George James Parfitt. 1870. John Hearn. 1871. Horatio Ward. 1872. James Henry Sloane. 1873. J. L. Whatley. 1874. Horatio Ward. 1875. 1876. John Chandler. 1877 1878. ,, 1879. ,, PROVINCIAL GRAND ASSISTANT DIRECTOR OF CEREMONIES. 1853. W. B. Sealy. 1854. 1855. 1856. 1857. C F. Marshall. 1858. J. Allen. 1859. John Elton Prower. 1860. 1861. 1862. H. Calf. 1863. 1864. D. A. Gibbs. 1865. J. Allen. 1866. ,, 1867. G. T. Dicks. 1868. — Gane. 1869. Horatio Ward. 1870. George Reynolds. 1871. Frederick Hastings Gold ney. PROVINCIAL GRAND POURSUIVANT. 1853. Samuel Hale Smith. I 1855. T. E. M. Marsh. 1854. C. W. Hind. I 1856. C. E. Owen. PROVINCIAL GRAND POURSUIVANT—continued.

1857. W. Biggs. 1858. R. Bradford. 1859. John Spencer. 1860. John Chandler. 1861. Rev. E. A. Jenkin. 1862. George Noyers. 1863. E. A. Moore. 1864. J. HoUway. 1865. W. L. Dore. 1866. Charles Feaviour. 1867. T. R. Lord. 1868. Horatio Ward.
PROVINCIAL GRAND ASSISTANT POURSUIVANT.
1869. Richard Tarrant. 1870. E. J. Inskip. 1871. W. Adye.
N. J. Cuss.
William Dean.
J. A. Lush.
Edwin Eyres.
W. S. Stodart.
Robert N. Fowler, M.P.
1878. F. Baldwin. 1879. H. E. Bishop.
1872.
1873.
1874.
1875.
1876.
1877.
1869. E. J. Inskip. 1870. J. Berry. 1871. Henry James Birch. 1872. T. G. Coal. 1873. Thomas E. Liddiard. 1874. J. V. Toone. PROVINCIAL GRAND STANDARD BEARER 1875. 1876. Walter H. Long, M.P.
1877.
1878. William Affleck.
1879.
1872. 1873. 1777.
R. L. White.
Edmund White.
1878.
1879.
  Thomas S.Futcher.
PROVINCIAL GRAND STEWARD. John Norton.
William Chubb.
Alexander Minty.
William Weeks.
George Scandover.
D. N. Keele.
1827. — Liley.
1853. T. Pain.
B. Robinson.
  C. E. Owen.
W. Whyte.
James Brown.
C. Brodie.
C. E. Owen.
W. Rogers.

Joseph Burt.
John Spencer.
1854.
1855. 1856. W. Biggs.
J. Long.
— Hopkins.
1857. G. Plummer.
J. Allen.
Alexander Bluoher Smith.
J. Long.
1858. Samuel Wittey.
T. A. Gibbs.
1859. James Edward Goddard Bradford.
John Chandler.
Thomas Chandler.
1860. James Edward Goddard Bradford.
William C. Merriman.
1861. Francis Stewart Wilmot.
PROVINCIAL GRAND 1861. George Noyers. 1862. Richard de M. Lawson. C. Parson. 1863. J. Toomer.
J. V. Westmacott.
William Hartley.
1864. J. Allen.
William Nott.
J. E. Hayward.
A. J. Marsh.
1865. S. G. Mitchell.
T. D. Taylor.
R. Pitt.
  Charles Feaviour.
1866. T. G. O'Reilly.
G. T. Dicks.
J. V. Westmacott.
A. L. Griffith.
1867. J. M. Cardell.
— Gane.
Horatio Ward.
1868. James Edward Goddard Bradford.
N. J. Cuss.
John Godwin.
— Wilton.
1869. Sir G. Goldney, Bart., M.P.
STEWARD—continued. 1869. Frederick Hastings Gold ney.
John Hearn.
Bartlett Little.
Thomas E. S. Jelley.
George Reynolds.
1870. Thomas Prideaux Saun ders.
Thomas Graham.

S. Saxty. *()*
E. B. Evans.
Jacoh Maggs.
J. C. Collie.
1871. W. T. Feltham.
Henry Merick.
Daniel Wiltshire.
Edwin Mellard Davis.
1872. James Haydon.
Horatio Dunn.
Samuel Carlton.
Thomas G. Clayton.
Edwin Browne.
William Dean.
1873. Frederick Baldwin. John Sylvester Turner. George Helps.
Edict against Freemasonry just issued by the Pope alluded to by P.G.M.
Reconsideration of P.G. Lodge Charity Rules and Fees.
Resignation of Sir Daniel
Gooch, Bart., M.P., as D.P.
G.M. after 16 years' tenure of that office, upon his being appointed a P.G.M. for
Berks and Bucks.
Installation of W. Brother S
Wittey as D.P.G.M. Presentation by the Brethren of the
Province of Wilts to Sir D.
Gooch, Bart., M.P., of the jewels and clothing of P.G.M.

Removal of the Lansdowne Lodge of Unity from Calne to Chippenham reported; con Becration of Lodge of Friend ship and Unity at Bradford on-Avon reported.

Addresses agreed to be presented to Her Majesty the
Queen, and to H.R.H. thi
Prince of Wales, upon the recovery of the iatter from a very dangerous illness. Gracious replies to the addresses received from Her
Majesty and the Prince ol
Wales.

LIST OF LODGES WORKING AT THE PRESENT TIME IN THE PROVINCE OF WILTSHIRE.

Lodge Of Rectitude, No. 335, Corsham.

Eoyal Sussex Lodge Of Emulation, No. 355, Swindon.

Elias De Derham Lodge, No. 586, Salisbury.

Lansdowne Lodge Of Unity, No. 626, Chippenham.

Lodge Of Concord, No. 632, Trowbridge.

Lodge Of Fidelity, No. 633, Devizes.

Lodge Of Friendship And Unity, No. 1271, Brad Ford-on-avon.

Gooch Lodge, No. 1295, New Swindon.

Longleat Lodge, No. 1478, Warminster.

Lodge Of Loyalty, No. 1533, Marlborough.

LODGE OF EECTITUDE, No. 335.

Warrant Dated 12th February, 1812.

Meets At The Methuen Arms Hotel, Corsham.

Lodges Held On The Last Tuesday In May And June,

At 3.30 P.m. Installation or The W. M. In June. Number Of Members Of The Lodge, 38, Of Whom 15 ARE P.M.

LODGE OF EECTITUDE.

This lodge is the oldest one in the Province acting under the same existing warrant, having held its meetings uninterruptedly for the last sixty-seven years, though its head-quarters have been frequently changed.

The original foundation of the lodge in this Province was caused by the transfer of the warrant from Lodge No. 16, at Norwich, to certain brethren at Westbury, formed into Lodge No. 632, the following being a copy of the Warrant:—

A.G.M.

"To All and Every Our Right Worshipful, Worshipful, and Loving Brethren, We, *Jftr&ncis* glatoion gtjitstings, (Earl *of* JJotra, garon gjaatinsa, 3t-tit2trfort, gtotwattlx. *Sic. &c. &c,*

Acting Grand Master, under the authority of His Royal Highness George No. 632. Augustus Frederick, Prince of Wales, &c. &c. &c, Grand Master of the most Ancient and Honourable Society of Free and

Accepted Masons, "Send Greeting.

"Whereas it appears by the Records of our Grand Lodge, that in the year 1724, a Warrant of Constitution was granted in due form, under the Seal of Masonry to certain Brothers therein named respectively Master Masons, for the purpose of holding a Lodge of the most Ancient and Honourable Society

of Free and Accepted Masons, and which was accordingly opened at the house known by the sign of the Queen's Head, in the city of Norwich, and was numbered 30: And whereas it also appears by the said Records, that upon the general alteration of numbers in the year 1740, the said Lodge became No. 27: That by the general alteration of numbers in the year 1756, it became No. 19: That upon the general alteration of numbers in the year 1781, it became No. 17: And that by the general alteration of numbers in the year 1792, it became No. 16; And whereas the Brethren resident at Norwich who composed the said Lodge had for many years neglected to communicate with the Grand Lodge or to contribute to the funds of the Society agreeable to the Laws of the Grand Lodge, and for which neglect they were apprized by repeated notices from the Grand Secretary that they would incur the censure of the Grand Lodge, but to such notices they paid no attention. The Grand Lodge did therefore on the 10th day of February, 1809, for such neglect and contempt declare the Brethren residing at Norwich to have forfeited their Eight and Title to the Warrant or Constitution of the said Lodge. And We by the authority in Us vested, and on the humble petition of our right trusty and wellbeloved William Vine, Samuel Bourne, Thomas Daniell, William James, Robert Watts, Jesse Greenland, James Bagley, and several other Brothers residing in or near the town of Westbury, in the county of Wilts, permission to assemble as a regular Lodge, have been pleased to assign the said Warrant of Constitution to the said Brethren, and they are accordingly hereby authorised to open and hold the said Lodge at the Crown Inn, in the town of Westbury aforesaid, under the denomination of the Lodge of Rectitude, and to be numbered 632 on the Registry of the List of Lodges, pursuant to the Order of the Grand Lodge on the said 10th day of February, 1809. And we do further at their said petition and of the great trust and confidence reposed in every of the said above-named Brethren, hereby appoint the said William Vine to be

Master, the said Samuel Bourne to be Senior Warden, and the said Thomas Daniell to be Junior Warden for opening the said Lodge, and for such further time only as shall be thought proper by the Brethren thereof: It being our will that this our appointment of the above officers shall in no wise affect any future election of officers of the said Lodge, but that such election shall be regulated agreeable to such Bye-laws of the said Lodge as shall be consistent with the general Laws of the Society, contained in the Book of Constitutions. And we will and require you the said William Vine to take special care that all and every the said Brethren are or have been regularly made Masons, and that they do observe, perform, and keep all the Rules and Orders contained in the Book of Constitutions. And further that you do from time to time cause to be entered in a book to be kept for that purpose an account of your proceedings in the Lodge together with all such Rules, Orders, and Regulations as shall be made for the good government of the same. That in no wise you omit once in every year to send to Us or our successors Grand Masters, or to his Royal Highness Augustus Frederick Duke of Sussex, our Deputy Grand Master, or to the Deputy Grand Master for the time being, an account in writing of your said proceedings and copies of all such Rules, Orders, and Regulations as shall be made as aforesaid, together with a List of the Members of the Lodge, and such a sum of money as may suit the circumstances of the Lodge and reasonably be expected towards the Grand Charity. Moreover we hereby will and require you the said William Vine as soon as conveniently may be to send an account in writing of what may be done by virtue of these presents.

"Given at London, under our Hand and Seal of Masonry, this 12th day of February, A.L. 5812, A.d. 1812.

"By the Grand Master's Command,

"glnnttsttts Jfrthmck, Jt.

"Witness, William H. White, G.S."

No records have as yet been discovered of the proceedings at Westbury, but from the first existing minutebook it appears that the lodge was suspended by the Grand Lodge after about four years' working, but that in the following year its Masonic duties were permitted to be resumed at Melksham, where it wandered from the King's Arms to the New Crown, to the Bear, and back again to the King's Arms. The brethren, however, did not get on with their neighbours any better than with their landlords, for we find that in 1829 official permission was sought for and obtained for the removal of the lodge to Box; because, amongst other reasons, "the inhabitants of Melksham evinced more than common opposition to the good cause of Masonry."

After a ten years' sojourn at Box, the lodge was removed to Monkton Farleigh as being nearer to Bath, where all the brethren resided, and on account of the Great Western Eailway, then recently made, passing through the former village, "making the neighbourhood there very unpleasant, and rendering the meetings exceedingly objectionable."

The brethren took up an active position in successfully opposing the endeavours of Grand Lodge, in 1845, to double the payments from the county lodges to the Fund of Benevolence, and Grand Lodge has never since renewed the proposal.

The first definite steps for memorialising the M.W. Grand Master to appoint a Provincial Grand Master for Wiltshire were taken by this lodge, with the happy result of which we are all aware.

In 1856 the lodge once more removed, and took up its quarters at the Methuen Arms Hotel, Corsham, where the brethren (who still are for the most part residents F of Bath) hold their meetings twice during the summer, and in goodly numbers carry on the duties of the craft in the true Masonic spirit of harmony and friendship.

The number of the lodge was originally 632; in 1813 it was changed to 639; in 1832 it became 420, and in 1863 it was altered to 335.

EXTRACTS FEOM THE MINUTE-BOOKS OF LODGE OF EECTITUDE. 1817. September 9. King's Arms, Melksham.

'' This evening the first lodge was held agreeably to summons, the business of the lodge having been suspended (until permission was obtained from the Grand Lodge to allow the lodge to resume its Masonic duties) in consequence of some irregularity in the proceedings of the lodge at Westbury." 1818. June 9.—Amongst the visitors was Brother Adey, the W.M. of Lodge Unity and Friendship, Brad-. ford, No. 564.

"1820. October 25.—Eesolved that a Lodge of Instruction be held every Sunday evening from 6 till 8." 1822. June 24.—At a meeting held at the New Crown Inn, it was agreed to meet in future in a private room, near the Church.

"1825. January 17.—Eesolved that the lodge be moved to the Bear Inn." 1825. May 9.—A petition was directed to be forwarded to H.E.H. the Duke of Sussex, the Grand Master of the United Fraternity of Ancient, Free, and Accepted Masons of England, for a Warrant of Dispensation to go in procession to Church on St. John's Day, the 24th of June.

1825. August 24.—A letter was received from the Grand Secretaries, William H. White and Edward Harper, informing the lodge of the appointment of John Eock Grosett, Esq., M.P., of Lacock Abbey, as Provincial Grand Master for Wilts. 1827. March 21.—A letter was received from the Marlborough Lodge respecting an address of condolenee to the M.W. Grand Master on the death of the M.W. Brother H.E. H. the Duke of York, but it was considered that it should emanate from the Provincial Grand Lodge.

"1827. May 19.—Eesolved to hold the meetings in future at the King's Arms Inn." 1827. June 25.—The W.M reported "that he had attended the Provincial Grand Lodge at Marlborough on 29th May. It had been determined to form a fund for the Province by each subscribing member paying an annual sum of 2s., with the addition thereto of a fee of 5s. from a Brother on his being 'made,' and Is. from a Brother on his joining." A subscription of £10 was raised in the lodge towards the

Provincial Grand Lodge furniture. A vote of thanks and a jewel were presented to P.M. Lazarus.

"Memorandum of officers appointed at the installation of P.G.M. J. E. Grosett, at Marlboro', 23rd October, 1827.

"J. E. Grosett, Provincial Grand Master.

Brother Eyres, P.G.S. Warden, W.M. Marlboro' Lodge.

„ Ames, P.G.J. Warden, W.M. Hindon Lodge.

„ J. Sheppard, P.G. Treasurer.

„ S. Lazarus, P.G. Eegistrar, P.M. Melksham Lodge.

„ Calley, P.G.S. Deacon.

„ Crowdy, P.G.J. Deacon.

„ Tucker, P.G. Secretary, W.M. Market Laving ton Lodge.,, Withers, P.G.D. of Ceremonies. „ William Noble, P.G. Supt. of Works, W.M.

Melksham Lodge. „ Filet, P.G. Chaplain.

Brother Phillips, P.G. Sword Bearer. „ Liley, P.G. Steward."

1828. March 5.—A letter was received from the P.G. Secretary, stating that the Masonic sermon preached at Marlboro' on 23rd October, 1827, was published. 1829. June 5.—An Emergency Lodge was held previous to the meeting of P. G. Lodge at Devizes this day. 1829. July 1.—A resolution was passed to apply to W. Brother William Euddle Browne, of Broad Hinton, Marlboro', the D.P.G. M. Wilts, for permission to move the lodge to Box, stating 'that the majority of the members resided in the city of Bath, that those resident in Melksham did not attend, that the landlord here threatened to turn the furniture into the street; and that, added to all this, the inhabitants evince more than common opposition to the good cause of Masonry.' 1829. July 12.—A resolution was passed to present Brother Joseph Berry with a jewel, in testimony of his zeal for the welfare of the lodge since its establishment at Melksham. 1829. August 12.—At a meeting held at the Queen's Head, Box, a communication was read from the P.G.M., containing his formal sanction of the removal of the lodge.

1835.—Extract from the *Freemasons' Quarterly Review* for 1835, p. 209, entered upon the Minutes as follows:—
"Several brethren have drawn our attention to the continued indisposition and necessary absence abroad of the E.W. Provincial Grand Master Brother Grosett, in consequence of which no Provincial Grand Lodge has been held for six years!! This Province was, till this unfortunate visitation of Providence, one of the most zealous and active in the crafty apathy has succeeded. In all societies the ruling authorities should remember how much their example determines the character of those over whom they preside. If the chief be active and courteous, the subordinates will be emulous and persevering.

"We earnestly but respectfully call the attention of the Deputy Grand Master of the Province of Wilts, whose private character has endeared him to all hearts, not to permit any longer delay, but to summon his brethren; they await but that summons to evince their former zeal, and prove that although the Tyler's sword has been long in the scabbard, it may yet gleam in the sunshine." 1836. May 17.—A resolution was passed "To write to the D.P.G.M. and inquire if he intended to hold a P.G. Lodge this summer: if not, they would, in co-operation with the other lodges of the Province, send a memorial seeking relief in this emergency to the Board of General Purposes." 1836. July 22.—A resolution was passed "That an humble address be presented to the Grand Master of Ireland, the Duke of Leinster, containing the best thanks of this lodge for his successful exertions in the House of Lords, in keeping inviolate the charter granted to the craft in the reign of George III., the exemption of Freemasons from the disabilities attending members of secret societies."

"Also that an address of congratulation be presented to H.E.H. the Duke of Sussex, Grand Master, on his late happy restoration to the blessings of sight. " 1837. May 19.—One guinea was voted to the subscription which was being raised for a testimonial to be presented to H.E.H. the Grand Master.

A vote of thanks was passed to Brother Drake for representing the lodge at the last Provincial Grand Meeting at Salishury.

A memorandum was made that fees due to the Provincial Grand Lodge were not paid, Brother Cooper, P.G. Secretary and Treasurer, having refused to receive any more money on account of the P.G. Lodge.

1838. June 1.—A printed communication from Dr. Crucifix was read, relative to the proposed asylum for aged and decayed Freemasons. 1838. July 27.—A committee was appointed to inquire into the subject of the removal of the lodge to the King's Head Inn, Monkton Farleigh, it being considered a more convenient place for meeting at, as all the members of the lodge resided at Bath. 1839. May 27.—The committee brought up their Eeport, recommending the removal of the lodge to Monkton Farleigh, which would be found almost as easy of access as Box, from the fact of the Bathford omnibus running within a mile of it, and Brother Parker's boats setting down at Claverton, which was about the same distance from Farleigh.

"Agreed that the expenses of Brother Drake in representing the lodge at the Provincial Grand Lodge of this Province, held at Salisbury, should be repaid him." 1839. June 19.—The following correspondence, which had taken place as to the removal of the lodge, was read:—

"To W. E. Browne, Esq., D.P.G.M. Province of Wilts, Broad Hinton, near Marlboro'.

"Eight Worshipful Sir and Brother,

"At the request of the members of the Lodge of Eectitude I have to solicit your assent to its removal from Box to Monkton Farleigh, three miles distant from the former place, and within your jurisdiction. The reasons why the members of the lodge would ask its removal are these: the room at Box is hy no means large enough to accommodate its increased numbers, added to which the neighbourhood has become very unpleasant in consequence of the Great Western Eailway passing through the village; the meeting held here last week was rendered exceedingly objectionable from the latter cause, whereas the place to which it is proposed the lodge shall be removed possesses the advantage of ample accommodation, is situated in a beautiful and retired spot, and rather nearer Bath—the residence of the members—than Box.

"May I request the favour of an early reply, that the necessary steps may be immediately taken to enable us to meet and instal our W.M. for the ensuing year on the 19th inst., on which occasion the brethren would be most happy to see you at the ceremony and banquet? "With every sentiment of regard,

"I am, Bight W. Sir and Brother, "Tours very fraternally, "Hinton East Drake, P.G.J.W. Pro. Wilts.

"To Hinton East Drake, Esq., P.G.J. W., 21, Broad Street, Bath.

"Dear Sir and Brother,

"In the absence of the D.P.G.M. (Mr. W. E. Browne) I beg to acknowledge the receipt of your letter to him, respecting the removal of the Lodge of Eectitude from Box to Monkton Farleigh. I am sorry the D.P.G.M. will not be returning from a tour on the Continent before the end of the present month, when he will have much pleasure in replying to your request. "I am, Dear Sir and Brother, "Yours fraternally,

"W. Browne."

"Broad Hinton Rectory, Marlboro'." 1840. May 8.—Met at the King's Head Inn, Monkton Farleigh, when the following letter from the D.P.G.M. was read:—

"Chisledon, Mariboko', "2nd July, 1839.

"Dear Sir and Brother,

"Having recently returned to England, I hasten to reply to your letter of the 3rd June, requesting me, as D.P.G. Master, to assent to the removal of the Lodge of Eectitude from Box to Monkton Farleigh.

"I see by the Book of Constitutions that the P.G. Master, or his Deputy, has the power to give or refuse the removal of a lodge from one town to another within his Province, and under the head of 'Eemoval of Lodges' the Master of the Lodge is required to send to the Provincial Grand Master, or his Deputy, a copy of the minutes of the lodge for removing, that it may be ascertained whether the law has been complied with, and that the removal be duly recorded.

"I shall be most happy in consenting to such a removal as may be conducive to the comforts and convenience of the Lodge of Eectitude, and the general encouragement of Masonry.

"I beg to thank the brethren most sincerely for their kind invitation, and hope at no distant period to do myself the pleasure of joining them.

"I am, Dear Sir and Brother, '' Yours very fraternally,

"W. E. Browne, D.P.G. Master, Wilts.

"To Hinton East Drake, Esq., P.G.J. "Warden, "21, Broad Street, Bath."

1841. June 21.—It was resolved that a memorial be sent to the D.P.G.M. of the Province, conveying the wish of the Lodge that a Provincial Lodge should be held during the present summer at Chippenham.

1842. May 9.—A letter received from the D.P.G.M. was read, stating his inability to hold a Provincial Grand Lodge during the year 1841 on account of his ill-health.

"Eesolution passed "That a respectful communication be sent to the P.G.M., Brother Grosett, showing the deplorable state of Freemasonry in the Province of Wilts, and asking his kind aid and assistance towards its revival.'" 1843. May 22.—A resolution was passed recording the heartfelt sorrow of the brethren at the muchlamented death of the E.W.G. M. the Duke of Sussex. Communication read from the Grand Lodge directing the usual Masonic mourning for twelve months, commencing 22nd April last. 1845. May 22.—A letter was read from the Grand Lodge stating that a resolution had been passed by which the payments from the country lodges to the Fund of Benevolence were to be increased from two to four shillings from each member. It was resolved unanimously that a formal protest should be presented to the Grand Lodge protesting against the confirmation of this resolu-

tion, and a committee was appointed to attend the Grand Lodge and vote against it. 1845. July 17.—A report was received from the committee who had attended the Grand Lodge, stating that the confirmation of the resolution to increase the fees to the Board of Benevolence had been rejected by a very large majority. 1852. July 16.—A resolution was passed "That the Secretary do communicate with the W.M.'s of the other lodges in the Province of Wilts to cooperate with them to memorialise the M.W. Grand Master to appoint a Provincial Grand Master for the Province of Wilts." 1853. May 12.—In conformity with the resolution passed at the last lodge, the W.M. reported that "he had been in communication with the Swindon Lodge (the only other lodge in Wiltshire now remaining) on the subject of the Provincial Grand Master, and he had reason to believe that a Provincial Grand Master had been appointed." 1856. May 7.—It was agreed to hold the lodge at the Queen's Head, Box, in future. 1859. Aug. 23.—It was agreed to remove the lodge to the Methuen Arms, Corsham.

The Eight Hon. Lord Methuen, P.G. M., and the Provincial Grand Lodge, were "received" by the Lodge.

1866.—The Provincial Grand Lodge was "received" by the Lodge. LIST OF WOBSHIPFUL MASTERS OF LODGE OF RECTITUDE.

Year. 1818. 1819. 1820. 1821. 1822. 1823. 1824. 1825. 1826. 1827. 1828. 1829. 1830. 1831. 1832. 1833. 1834. 1835. 1836. 1837. 1838. 1839. 1840. 1841. 1842. 1843. 1844. 1845. 1846. 1847. 1848. 1849.

Worshipful Master.
Thomas Burrough Smith
John Nalder
　Francis Fricker
Joseph Berry
John Nalder.
Samuel M. Lazarus
　» »
　William Noble
J. Liley
James Noble
Uinton East Drake
　John Johnson

Gilbert Elliot Mitchell
James Wedderspoon
Joseph Govey
George Baker Keeling
Samuel Cooper
Samuel Bennett.
Richard Westall.
J. W. Fraser
Bartlett Little
Augustus George Barrette
Henry Lacy Yea.
John Broadley
Robert Skinner
G. M. Temple
Dr. James Tunstall
Thomas Steele
Rev. John Somerville Broderip
« No. of Meetings
Year. Worshipful Master.. of the Lodge.

1850. Charles Haselar 2 1851. John Broadley 2 1852. „ 2 1853. F. T. Allen (Mayor of Bath)... 2 1854. A. Smallbone 2 1855. George Firmin 2 1856. E. F. Collings 2 1857. Horatio Jamea 2 1858. Edmund White...... 2 1859. — Oliver 2 1860. C. F. Marshall 2 1861. E. Turner Payne 2 1862. — King 2 1863. J. Hollway 2 1864. Samuel Hayward 2 1865. William Gibbs 2 1866. S. G. Mitchell...... 2 1867. Major J. Randle Ford 2 1868. John Elkington Gill 2 1869. Thomas Robert Lord 2 1870. Alfred A. Mitchell 2 1871. Jacob Maggs 2 1872. James Henry Sloane 2 1873. Colonel Henry Joseph Guyon... 2 1874. Francis Burnitt 2 1875. „ 2 1876. William Adolphus Rolfe.... 2 1877. Frederick Baldwin..... 2 1878. Frederick D. Gardner 2 1879. Alfred Fudge 2 EOYAL SUSSEX LODGE OF EMULATION, No. 355.

Warrant Dated 1819.

Meets At The Masonic Hall, Swindon.

Lodges Held On The Friday Nearest The Full Moon

In Each Month, At 6 P.m. Installation Of The W.M. In December. Number Of Members Of The Lodge, 72, Of Whom 21 ARE P.M.

EOYAL AECH OHAPTEE.

Warrant Dated February 6th, 1856.

Meets At The Masonic Hall, Swindon.

Chapters Held On The Friday Nearest The Full Moon In January, February, October, NovemBer, And December, At 4 P.m.

Installation Of Principals Du The Month Of December.

Number Of Members Of The Chapter, 29, Of Whom 11 Are P.Z.

ROYAL SUSSEX LODGE OF EMULATION.

The number of the lodge upon the books of the Grand Lodge was originally 702, which was altered in 1832 to 453, and in 1863 was brought forward to 355. The absence of the minute-books, from the commencement of the lodge in 1818 down to 1852, causes a loss of information, which, however, is to some extent supplied by the lodge register of members, with the dates of their joining or initiation and amount of the fees paid by them for the years 1818 to 1827, both inclusive, from which it appears that the lodge met at the Goddard Arms Inn, Swindon, and that there were between twenty and thirty members, including Brothers T. CaUey, M.P., of Burdrop Park, Eev. D. Williams, of Avebury House, and Eichard Miles, of Morden House; and also by a packet of old letters and papers kindly lent by Brother John Chandler, P.P.S.G.W., of which the following are copies or references:—

The draft petition, dated 1818, to the Grand Master for a Warrant of Constitution for the new lodge, to be called the "Lodge of Emulation," to be held at the Goddard

A HISTORY OF FREEMASONRY, ETC. 81

Arms Inn, Swindon, on the first Friday in every month. Robert Withers to be the first W.M.; Samuel Sheppard to be the first S.W.; and Wm. Gerring the first J.W.

Applied for by—

John H. Sheppard, Elm Tree Inn, Devizes, 341; William Morse Crowdy, Foundation Lodge, 121, Abingdon; Eobert Withers, Lodge of Virtue, 811, Bath; John Wyatt, Elm Tree Inn, Devizes, 341; Samuel Sheppard, Elm Tree Inn, Devizes, 341; John Osborne, Elm Tree Inn, Devizes, 341; William Ger-

ring, Foundation Lodge, 121, Abingdon.

1818. April 28.—A letter from the Grand Secretary to Eobert Withers, enclosing dispensation for holding a lodge, and with Book of Constitution and jewels. "swindon, *May 1th,* 1818. Lodge Of Emulation, No. 702.

"Dear Sir and Brother,

"As we have received a dispensation from the *Grand Lodge,* authorising us to meet as *Masons,* and as the Worshipful Master of the Lodge of Virtue, of Bath, who recommended and presented the petition, has fixed for Monday, the 11th inst., for *Installation* at 10 o'clock in the forenoon, at the Goddard Arms Inn, Swindon, the pleasure of your company, with as many brethren of the Devizes Lodge as can conveniently attend, is particularly requested. 'Your favour per return of post stating how many brethren will favour us with their company (for the information of the Steward) will much oblige, "Dear Sir and Brother, "Yours truly,

"Samuel Sheppard."

"Mr. Williams, Devizes." ii S 1819. November 1.—A letter from the Grand Secretary to the W.M. of the Lodge:—

"London, Feeemasons' Hall, *November 1st,* 1819. "W. Master,

"The Warrant of Constitution for your Lodge having been signed by our M.W. Grand Master the Duke of Sussex, we beg leave to say that the dispensation under which you are now working is no longer of any force or virtue, and that upon its being returned to us the warrant shall be immediately forwarded in lieu thereof.

"We are, W. Master,

"Your faithful Servants and Brothers, "william H. White,) "edward Harper, J "The Master of the Lodge of Emulation, Swindon." 1819. A Royal Arch Chapter was probably attached to the lodge in 1819, from the following passage in a letter from Thomas Harper to Brother Eobert Withers, dated 207, Fleet Street, London, 13th March, 1819, relating to a silver chaplain's jewel and collar forwarded to him for the lodge:—
" The articles sent by Brother Geming I hope were approved; should any others

be wanting for the other companions of the Eoyal Arch, it will afford me pleasure to forward them to your order."
1825. May 27.—A letter from the Grand Secretary, E. Harper, acknowledging remittances, and enclosing Grand Lodge certificates for two brethren.
1825. August 23.—A letter from the Grand Secretaries announcing the appointment of J. E. Grosett, M.P., of Lacock Abbey, as P.G.M. 1826. November 25.—A letter from J. R. Grosett, P. G.M., announcing a Provincial Grand Lodge meeting at the Bear Hotel, Devizes, on the 12th day of December, and requesting the attendance of the W.M. to introduce to him the brethren of his lodge. 1827. May 11.—A letter from J. E. Grosett, P.G.M., that he had presented to H.E.H. the Duke of Sussex the address of condolence from this lodge on the death of the Duke of York, which H. E.H. our M.W.G. Master had graciously received, and transmitted to him the enclosed written answer with his Eoyal Highness's signature:—

"To the Worshipful Master, Officers, and Brethren of the Eoyal Sussex Lodge of Emulation, No. 702, Swindon.

"Brethren,

"Accept of my warmest thanks for your sincere condolence and sympathy on the loss which the nation, the craft, and myself have sustained by the decease of my much-lamented and beloved brother his Eoyal Highness the Duke of York, a Past Deputy Grand Master of our Order. I most sincerely feel your kind expressions on the occasion, which afford me an additional proof of the deep participation our community takes in the interests of every one of its members.

"I avail myself of this occasion to assure you of my good-will towards your lodge, and of my unceasing anxiety for the honour, credit, and happiness of the craft at large.
(Signed) "augustus Frederick, G.M.

"Kensington Palace, April 14, 1827. " 1827. June 20.—A letter from S. M. Lazarus, W.M. and Z. Eoyal Sussex (?of Bath), 69, addressed to M. Crowdy, W.M.:— 6, Abbey Street, Bath, *June*

20th, 1827. "W. Sir and Brother,

"I had the honour of an interview with our P.G.M. yesterday, and find that he expected to have received communications from the several lodges, stating who and how many are desirous of taking offices in the P.G.L., and then he will select those whom he thinks most proper to fill them, and I imagine the Senior Masters will take the Senior Offices. He is further desirous of knowing if the brethren of the lodges generally are satisfied with the arrangements made in the P.G.L. hy the Masters and Wardens, namely, to pay 2s. annually and fees, as that was agreed to only by the officers; he therefore wishes to know if the same met the approbation of the brethren of the respective lodges. Now, my dear sir, I know you will excuse me in suggesting to you what I think is most advisable: for each lodge to write to the P.G.M. and state how many of the brethren will accept offices, but not to name what offices, and at the same time-that the brethren, if so, gave their assent to what was done in the P. G.L., &c, &c.

"I trust that you will not forget to name Brother Vilet with the list of P.G. L. officers.

"I beg to acquaint you that the Royal Sussex Chapter will meet on Sunday, the 1st July, at eleven o'clock A.m., and the Knights will assemble at six o'clock in the evening, for the purpose of making KnightTemplars. There are several brethren from Hinton, Lavington, and I expect four from Marlboro', to be exalted. This you will please to acquaint Brother Brown, who expressed a desire to visit, and should any brethren of your lodge wish to take one or both of the above degrees, shall be most happy to confer it upon them; if so, have the kindness to inform me by Monday's post, as all the notices must be sent by that time. You must inform me all particulars of candidates for exalting same as initiation, namely, age, &c., &c.

"Shall be happy to see you on the occasion, and any other brethren of your lodge, to whom I beg you will present my fraternal respects, and accept the same from,

""Worshipful Sir and Brother,

"Yours very Masonically, "S. M. Lazaeus, W.M. and 2.E. Sussex, 69. "M. Crowdy, Esq., Swindon." 1827. December 27.—A letter from E. Tucker, P.G. Secretary, announcing that at the P.G.L. held at the Guildhall, Marlboro', on the 23rd October, "it was resolved unanimously that each lodge within the Province should make a return of its members to the P.G. Secretary similar to those made to the Grand Lodge, with the following payments; namely, for every contributing member, Is.; for every joining brother, Is.; and for every initiation since 29th May last, 5s. " 1828. January 5.—A letter from the Grand Secretary as to arrears of quarterages due.
1829. August 10.—A letter from W. E. Browne, D.P.G.M., resigning office of W.M. 1829. November 19.—A letter from Eobert Tucker, P.G. Secretary, asking for return of members pursuant to the Twelfth Article of P.G. Bye-Laws. 1830. January 30.—A letter from the Grand Secretary for contributions to the Lodge of Benevolence which were overdue. 1830. February 6 —A letter from the P.G.M. to the D.P.G.M.:—

"Clifton, *February 6th,* 1830.

"Dear Sir and Brother,

"In reply to your letter I accede with pleasure to the application of the W.M. , Officers, and Brethren of the Eoyal Sussex Lodge of Emulation, No. 702, Swindon, for holding their lodge on the Friday nearest the full moon, instead of the first Friday in each month, as heretofore. It will he necessary that you notify the change of the day to the Grand Secretary.

"I am happy to hear the Lodge of Union at Salisbury is prospering. In the event of the dedication of a new hall there, I think it will be advisable to hold our Provincial Meeting at that place.

"I hope the Lodge of Eectitude, removed from Melksham to Box, goes on well. I am not aware whether the new lodge at Trowbridge, for which I obtained the warrant some time ago, but which could not be delivered to them by the G.S. until they completed the requisite conditions depending on themselves, have yet received it, but I suppose so, and hope they will prosper.

"I am, Dear Sir and Brother,

'' Yours fraternally,

"J. E. Grosett, P.G.M. Wilts.

"W. R. Browne, Esq., D.P.G.M., Wilts." 1830. December 27.—A letter from John James Calley resigning membership.

1831. October 12.—A letter from the Grand Secretaries, William H. White and Edward Harper, applying for contributions to the Fund of Benevolence, which was in arrear. 1833. April 8.—A Letter addressed to " Mr. Eobert Withers, Eoyal Sussex, 453, Swindon," from the Grand

Secretary, E. Harper, with, receipt for quarterage, and relative to dispensation for initiating a person under age to be granted by the P.G.M. or the D.P.G.M. 1834. May 9.—A copy of the return made to the Clerk of the Peace, pursuant to Act 39 George III., by Eobert Withers, W.M., mentions that Lodge No. 453 meets at the Goddard Arms Inn, on Friday nearest the full moon in each month. 1834. July 21.—A letter from Henry Cooper, of Salisbury, P.G.S., asking for Eeturns previous to arranging for a meeting of the P.G.L. 1835. Sept. 11.—A letter from the Grand Secretaries, White and Harper, for Eeturns of members. 1837. October 1.—A letter from W. E. Browne, D.P.G.M., to Eobert Withers, W.M., relative to arrangements for the P.G.L. to be held on the 6th at Swindon. 1837. October 6.—Bough minutes of the Provincial Grand Lodge held at the Goddard Arms (No. 453 being the Eeceiving Lodge) by the D.P.G.M. The Address of congratulation to the E.W.G.M., H.E.H. the Duke of Sussex, on the recovery of his sight, agreed to at the last lodge, was read, and also the letter containing H.E.H.'s most gracious reply.

Appointment of P.G. Officers:—W. M. Crowdy, P.G.S.W.; J. James Calley, J. W.; Eev. J. Greenly, Chap.; E. Withers, Eegistrar; H. Cooper, Secretary; Samuel Cooper, S.D.; Samuel Bennett, J.D.; John Brown, D. of C.; W. Brown, Sup. of W.; W. Goodenough, Sword Bearer; J. H. Sheppard, re-elected Treasurer.

Brother S. M. Lazarus, as he now lived a great distance from the Province, declined to accept office, and the D.P. G.M. conferred upon him, in consideration of the great services he had rendered to Masonry in the Province, and his regular attendance at the P.G.L.'s, the privilege of taking the rank and wearing the clothing of a P.P.G.W. in the Province of Wilts.

1840. March 9.—The resignation of membership by J. J. Calley, addressed to E. Withers. 1843. February 20.—A letter from G. S. White to Brother 0. Eeynolds, relative to votes for the Girls' School. 1843. December 26.—A letter from the D.P.G.M. relative to his inability to accept the invitation to their banquet, and mentioning that " two noblemen had been proposed to fill the chair of the late G.M.—the Earl of Zetland and the Marquis of Salisbury—and that the latter was expected to withdraw.
" 1848. February 4.—A letter from J. Browne acknowledging letter of condolence on the death of William Puddle Browne, the D.P.G.M. 1852. September 13.—A letter from Minard C. Eea, W. M. Lodge 453, to the Monkton Farleigh Lodge, stating that the members of the lodge had come to the same conclusion as the members of that lodge as to the necessity of having a P.G.M. for this Province, and that "most of the chief officers of the defunct P.G. Lodge of Wiltshire are members of this, and claim it as their mother lodge, and are most anxious to have it renewed again.
" 1852. November 13.—A letter from James Smith, W.M. of Salisbury Lodge, disapproving of the revival of the P.G. L. on the ground of the expense it would entail, on the small number of lodges in the Province, and of the distance intervening between the lodges in this county. EXTEACTS FROM THE MINUTE-BOOKS OF EOYAL SUSSEX LODGE OF EMULATION.

"1852. November 26.—The brethren appeared in Masonic mourning for the death of that distinguished Brother, F. M. the Duke of Wellington. The W.M. brought before the lodge the subject of petitioning the M.W.G.M. to appoint a P.G.M. for this Province, and letters on

the subject were read from the Salisbury and Monkton Farleigh Lodges."

"1853. February 11.—A petition to the M.W.G.M. to appoint a P.G.M. agreed to and signed." 1853. April 6.—An announcement was made that the office of P.G.M. for Wiltshire had been offered by the M.W.G.M. to the Eight Hon. Lord Methuen, and accepted by him.

1865. An application was made by William Millar for assistance, "he being a brother who had been confined as a prisoner for debt in the Queen's Prison for upwards of forty-seven years, and who was now about to be discharged therefrom." £2 2s. was subscribed towards the fund being raised for him. 1862. January 17.—The W.M. reported that he had attended the special Grand Lodge held at Freemasons' Hall on the 8th inst., on the occasion of an address of condolence to her Majesty being agreed to upon the melancholy occasion of the recent death of H.E.H. the Prince Consort. 1862. December 30.—A proposal was made for a subscription to the fund for relief of the distress in Lancashire. 1863. September 16.—A letter from the Grand Secretary was read, stating that the Grand Lodge had resolved to alter the number of lodges on the register, so that the numbers of all lodges might be brought forward in regular succession, and that this lodge would thenceforth stand on the register of the Grand Lodge as No. 355. 1864. December 9.—The resignation of J. H. Sheppard as Treasurer was received. "He had been a member of the lodge and held the office of Treasurer from its commencement; he was made a Master Mason at the Devizes Lodge, May 3rd, 1817; he made application to the Grand Master for this lodge when the first meeting took place on May 1st, 1818; he attended a Masonic meeting at Bath on September 23rd, 1819, to witness the Duke of Sussex consecrate the new Masonic Hall, when about 700 brethren attended. He attended the first Provincial Grand Lodge held at Salisbury, October 27th, 1827, when he was appointed P.G. Treasurer, and has been a subscribing member of this lodge from its commencement."

"1867. October 8.—The Provincial Grand Lodge was received by this lodge."

"1869. March 31.—The Provincial Grand Lodge was received by this lodge at the New Hall, Chippenham." 1870. October 17.—£3 3s. voted for the relief fund for the sick and wounded in the Franco-Prussian war.

LIST OF WOESHIPFUL MASTEES OF EOYAL SUSSEX LODGE OF EMULATION.

Year.

1818. 1819. 1820. 1821. 1827. 1829. 1833. 1834. 1835. 1836. 1837. 1848. 1849. 1850. 1851. 1852. 1853. 1854. 1855. 1856. 1857. 1858. 1859. 1860. 1861. 1862. 1863. 1864. 1865. 1866. 1867. 1868. 1869. 1870. Worshipful Master.

Robert Withers

John James Calley.

M. Crowdy

William Ruddle Browne

Robert Withers

J. W. Browne

John Elton Prower.

Davenport W. Collyns

Minard C. Rea

Sir Daniel Gooch, Bart., M.P,

W. F. Gooch.

Thomas E. M. Marsh

Rev. George Campbell

Edward Robert Ing.

C. W. Hind.

Thomas Chandler.

John Chandler

Richard Bradford.

William Read.

John Toomer.

Henry Kinneir

Joseph Wentworth.

W. H. Tarrant

R. S. Edmunds

Alexander James Braid

Richard Tarrant

John Godwin.

No. of Meetings of the Lodge.

7 3 8 19 10

7

9

10

8

8

9

8

10 10

9

9

9

11

8

10

9

Year. Worshipful Master.

1871. Henry C. Tombs. 1872. John Toomer. 1873. ,, ,,... 1874. Thomas G. Coall. 1875. Alfred Plummer 1876. William Affleck 1877. T. E. Liddiard 1878. J. Campbell Maclean 1879. William Jenkins

No. of Meetings of the Lodge.

9

8

9

. 10

11

12

11

10

9

LODGE ELIA8 DE DEEHAM, No. 586.

Warrant Dated 1851. Meets At The Masonic Hall, Salisbury. Lodges Held On The Second Thursday In Each Month, At 7 P.M.

Installation Of The W.M. In January. Number Of Members Of The Lodge, 56, Of Whom 12 Are P.M.

EOTAL AECH CHAPTER.

Warrant Dated August 7th, 1867.

Meets At The Masonic Hall, Salisbury.

Chapters Held On The Third Friday In January,

March, August, September, And November,

At 7 P.m.

Installation Of The Principals On The Third Friday

In September. Number Of Members Of The Chapter, 28, Of Whom 4 Are P. Z.

LODGE ELIAS DE DERHAM.

The date of the present Warrant does not indicate the real antiquity of this lodge, which has practically been in existence for a century and a half, although, owing to a temporary suspension of its working, the original Warrant

was lost.

From the minute-books, commencing in 1732, and from the collection of Masonic documents and letters of the late Brother Michael Burrough, we find that Salisbury formerly took a very active interest in Masonry, that there were several lodges in full work in that city at the same time, and that their meetings were frequent and their rules strict.

The number of visitors from London attending the Salisbury Lodge appears to have been unusually large, and the mention of the various inns and taverns at which their own lodges were held recalls to mind several past celebrities who were in the habit of frequenting them, as referred to in the "History of Sign-boards." Thus, amongst the visitors there were, in 1738, "Thomas Clark from the Bull's Head, Southwark," an inn where the Artists' Club used to meet, of which Hogarth was a member.

In 1742 "James Wallace, of the Fountain in Cattern

Street, in the Strand." This house was famous as the meeting-place of the ultra-loyal party in 1685, who here talked over public affairs before the meeting of Parliament. Eoger Lestrange, who had been recently knighted by the King, took a leading part in these consultations. But in the reign of George II. this same house became a great resort for the Whigs. The KitCat Club used to meet at this house: it consisted of thirty-nine distinguished noblemen and gentlemen attached to the Protestant succession of the House of Hanover, including the Dukes of Eichmond, Devonshire, Marlborough, Somerset, Grafton, Newcastle, and Dorset; the Earls of Sunderland and Manchester; also Steele, Addison, Congreve, Garth, Vanbrugh, Mainwaring, Stepney, Walpole, and Pulteney. Tonson, the Honorary Secretary, was presented with portraits of all the members. The name of the club was derived from that of the first landlord of the tavern, Christopher Cat; he excelled in the making of mutton-pies, which were named after him Kit Cat, and were the standard dish of the club. The portraits which were presented to Tonson are now hung in Willis's Eooms, King Street, St. James's, London, in the suite of rooms occupied by the Prince of Wales Lodge, No. 259 (of which the writer is a member), at whose banquets the customary mutton-pies still regularly appear.

In 1742, "P. Swanton, of the Bear, Strand, London." At this tavern the earliest meetings of the Society of Antiquaries took place, commencing November 5th, 1707.

The Salisbury Lodge commenced its meetings at the Three Lions Inn, whence they removed three years afterwards, by permission of the Grand Master, to the Mitre and Crown.

In 1766 Brother Cooper presented a jewel and a seal, engraved with the Masons' arms, for the use of the lodge, which they still possess, and a few years afterwards he added a pair of candlesticks.

The lodge removed, in 1769, to a private room at Mr. Lush's, in High Street.

In 1776 commenced a lengthy correspondence with the Grand Lodge upon the subject of their application for a contribution towards the building and furnishing their new hall, ending in the erasure of the Salisbury Lodge for non-compliance with the application; but a compromise was subsequently effected, and the lodge was restored to its former position; but again in 1800 a controversy arose with the Grand Lodge with regard to a compulsory subscription to be annually paid by every Mason towards liquidating the debts of the Grand Lodge, which also resulted in the erasure of the lodge again; whereupon it was resolved to form a Grand Lodge in Salisbury, independent of the Grand Lodge of England, but this was never carried into effect, and the Salisbury Lodge died out in 1809.

The Lodge of Union, No. 819, received the Provincial Grand Lodge in 1828; and there is an account for the following year with the P.G. Treasurer showing that there were then 29 members of the lodge, including Sir J. P. Milbanke, Bart. Some of their working tools are in the possession of Lodge Elias de Derham, but when the Union Lodge ceased to exist, and why, is not

quite clear.

Until the present lodge was constituted in 1851, there had been none for many years at Salisbury, but happily the Elias de Derham is established on a firm foundation of zealous brethren, who by their endeavours to promote the welfare of Freemasonry do their utmost to make up for the lukewarmness of past years. There are now several orders of Craft and Christian Masonry attached to this lodge.

EXTEACTS FKOM THE MINUTE-BOOKS OF THE SALISBURY LODGE.

"1732. January.—Paid the Deputy Grand Master for charity money, and the Secretary for getting dispensation, £2 12s. 6d. Paid for jewels, £1 15s. Compasses, 7s. Gloves when Brother Legg was made, 8s. Constitutionbook, 4s. Two lodge-books, 9s. Grinding the sword. Aprons, 13s."

"1732. 11th Dec—At a meeting of the Society of Free and Accepted Masons for the settling and constituting of a lodge, pursuant to a dispensation from and under seal of the Eight Hon. Lord Montague, Present Grand Master, for the constitution of a lodge for the city of New Sarum, in the county of Wilts, regulations and bye-laws were agreed and consented unto."

"1732. 27 Dec.—At a constitution of a regular lodge of Free and Accepted Masons at the house of Brother Edward Eandall, situate in the city of New Sarum, and called by the name of the Three Lyons Inn, on Wednesday, the 27th day of December, in the year of Masonry 5732, the following orders and bye-laws for the better regulating and governing the said lodge were by the master, wardens, and brethren of the said lodge agreed unto:—

"Vizt. That no persons shall be admitted members of the said lodge unless first balloted for by all the brethren of the said lodge, and chosen *nemine contradicente,* and that upon such balloting no brother shall presume to ask another who he balloted for, whether for or against.

"Item. That no persons on a lodge night shall presume to supp in the lodge-room. But in case they shall have

a mind to eate shall withdraw to another room.

H

"Item. That the Jewells and the materiall furniture of the said lodge shall not be removed out of the lodge to mate any person or persons Masons in private, and that noe number of the brethren sufficient to form a lodge doe presume to admitt any person or persons Masons in private.

"Item. That no proposalls either for beautifying the lodge or disposition of money or other things shall be without the generall consent of the brotherhood, *nem. eon.* "Item. The days for making att the said lodge are appointed to be the first and third Wednesday in every month, to be present at six of the clock in the evening, and brake up to close the lodge at ten in the evening.

"Item. That all persons who are intended to be admitted brethren of this lodge shall be the first lodge night proposed to the Society, and the next lodge night balloted for.

"Item. If any brother shall propose a person to be balloted for, and the Society shall accept the said person as a member, if, after he is so accepted, he shall refuse to appear to be initiated, the person proposing Tiim shall pay half the expense that would have been in the making.

"Item. That the quarteridge money to be paid for the subsistence of the said lodge be eight shillings per quarter, and that in case any brother shall depart from Sarum, upon a week's notice to be given to master or wardens, such brother shall be excused paying, provided absent above two months.

"James Drake, Master. Will. Hillman. Jos. Mede, Senr. Warden. G. Nicholas.

Hen. Younger, Junr. Warden. Jno. Case.

Wm. Legg. James Case.

Edwd. Eandall. Theod. Burleton." 1733. August 27.—At this meeting the following visitors were present:—His Grace the Duke of Eichmond and the Hon. Mr. Fox.

1733. Dec. 19.—John Burrough was made a Mason.

"1734.—The fee for making a brother £3 3s. Od. Paid for gloves for making Blake, 4s. 9d."

"1735. Oct. 1.—Visitors: Gilbert Douglas, Bear and Harrow; Thos. Stakes, Two Angels and Crown."

"Oct. ye 15th, 1735. Ann. Lithotomorum, 5735.—At a meeting then held it was proposed to allow the Secretary the usual stipend pay'd by other lodges for the minutes of the quarterly communication, which proposal passed in the affirmative. Proposed that a petition to Grand Master or Deputy Grand Master, setting forth the reasons for removing from Brother Eandall's to Brother Davenport's, and praying for a confirmation of such removal and an alteration in the future lodge-books, be forthwith drawn, and that Brother Douglas, visitor now present, do carry and present such petition, signed by the brethren of this lodge, to the Grand Master, or in his absence his Deputy; Brother Douglas promising to take care thereof and transmit it with the Grand Master or his Deputy's answer thereto with all speed suitable to the occasion.

"Chas. Hooton. James Drake, M.

Geo. Baily, F.C. John Burrough, D.S. W.

Will. FfusseU. Chas. Blake, D.J.W.

Hen. Davenport. John Corfe." *Visiting Brother.*—Gilbert Douglas.

"Jan. ye 7th, 1735.— At a meeting then held Brother Douglas (to whom it had been recommended) reported to the lodge that he had acquainted Brother Martin Clare (who transacts all business for the Grand Master in his absence) with the ill usage we had received from Brother Eandall, and our having thereupon removed the lodge to the Mitre and Crown, in the city of New Sarum; whereupon Brother Clare was pleased to approve of our reasons and conduct, and to order the Three Lyons to be erased out of the lodge-book, and the Mitre and Crown substituted in the room thereof; he representing to said Brother Clare that we were willing to allow the stipend allotted to the Secretary upon his transmitting us constantly the minutes of the quarterly communication; the Secretary was thereupon or-

dered to transmit them constantly; and Brother Douglas, paying the Secretary's fees, brought us the minutes of the two last quarterly communications. It being further moved by said Brother Douglas that being at such a distance from London we were not able, without great inconvenience, to attend the quarterly communications by our master and wardens in person, Brother Clare was pleased to indulge us in the liberty of attending the quarterly communications by proxy, that proxy being entered a member of this lodge; and it being proposed that thanks should be returned to Brother Douglas for his care and conduct herein, and that he should be admitted a member of this lodge, and further desired to act as proxy to the master of the lodge at the ensuing or any future quarterly communication (the master or wardens of this lodge not being then in London), and on account of such his service and attendance his quarterages here to be excused, all which was agreed to, *nem. con.;* and Brother Douglas having accepted thankfully of such admission and proxyship, he has accordingly enrolled himself a member of this lodge."

"1735. January 15.—Eeceived for passing fellow craft of Brother Crawford, 5s."

"1737. Aug. 3.—Eeceived of Brother Dore for passing master, 5s."

"1738. Aug. 5.—Visitor: Thomas Clark, from the Bull's Head, Southwark."

"1738. Dec. 27.—Visitor: Eobert Fulton, of the Sun in Holborn, London. "

"1739. March 7.—Fee for 'making' raised to two guineas."

"1740.—Paid for ye peddestall, £1 14s."

"1742. Jan. 20.—Visitor: James Wallace, of the Fountain in Cattern Street, in the Strand."

"1742. March 17.—Visitors: P. Swanton, Bear, Strand, London; Josh. Southerton, Three Tuns, Newgate Street."

"1744. June 24.—Paid for a ribbon for Secretary's jewel, 2s. Paid for a square, Is."

"1745. June 24.—Visitors: John Anderson, The George, St. Mary Ax; Eichard Yates, Bull's Head, White Chappie; Eichard Winston, King's Arms, Tower Street; John Harrington, Anchor and Baptist's Head, Chancery Lane. Paid for ribbon for Master's Jewell, 11s. 6d."

"1746. Oct. 19.—At this lodge *were made Scotts Masons,* five brethren of the lodge" (including the W.M. Staples).

"1746. Dec. 27.—Being the anniversary feast of St. John, Brother Morris, having been before duly elected, was then *installed* Master. Hitherto the Master had been ' chosen,' and no mention was made of installation. Paid for Treasurer's Jewell, 8s. Paid for washing cloth and two hammers, 2s. Paid for two pairs of compasses, lOd."

"1747. Nov. 4.—Visitor: Thos. Clark, Bull's Head, Southwark. Paid for ribbon for Treasurer's jewell, 3s."

"1749. Dec. 27.—Paid for the table and print, £1 lIs. 6d." 1758. Aug. 8.— Extraordinary Lodge for the reception of two visiting brethren from France, Brother De Court and Brother Guerin. 1762. July.—The lodge was removed to the Plume of Feathers. 1763. July.— The lodge was removed to the Maidenhead.

"1765. April 5.—Paid for painting the cloth, Is.; for cleansing the aprons, 5s."

"1766. Jan. 16.—Eobert Cooper, of Sarum, was made a Mason. Paid for twenty-four books of lodges, 12s.; for a green cloth, 14s."

"1766. Jan. 15.—Agreed that no person for the future shall be made a Mason without paying two guineas and a crown, and if desirous to be made not of a lodge night, to pay one guinea over and above two guineas and a crown."

"1766. Feb. 19.—Brother Edgar reported that he had paid the two guineas as directed, and produced the Grand Secretary's receipt for the same for charity to the Grand Lodge, and two-shillings and sixpence for an alteration on the removal of the lodge."

"1766. March 19.—Agreed by unanimous consent that the grateful thanks of the lodge be given to Brother Cooper for the magnificent presents and regard he has to the lodge, to wit, a jewell with gold lace, and a seal engraved with the Masons' arms for the use of the lodge. " 1766. April 3.—The Eight Hon. Lord Blaney, Eight Worshipful Grand Master of Masons, was received with all honour and respect due to him.

"1766. April 16.—Agreed that each brother should subscribe double for this quarter, in order to help defray the expenses extraordinary which were expended in the reception of the Eight Hon. Lord Blaney. Paid for expenses at this extra lodge, £7 Is. 8d.; paid Mr. Lush for a chair and throne, £5 10s. 6d.; paid Brother Hamley for lace, £2 3s. 4d. "

"1767. Oct. 21.—Paid for the Past Master's jewel, £1 5s. Letters from the last quarterly communication of the Grand Lodge were read." 1768. Oct. 19. —Eichard Eighley, of Wilton, a. Quaker, was proposed to be made a Mason. 1768. Nov. 30.—The Eight Worshipful Master communicated to the lodge some resolutions and minutes of the Grand Lodge, craving certain assistances to further a scheme for incorporating the Society under the title and advantages to be mentioned in such charter of incorporation. The same was referred to future consideration. 1769. March 20.—At this meeting notice was received from the Grand Lodge of a committee of charity to be held at the Horn Tavern, in Fleet Street, the 20th of April, and a quarterly communication to be held at the Crown and Anchor Tavern, in the Strand, the 28th inst., in which was enclosed a scheme for the incorporation of Masons to be considered, and the sense of this lodge to be, by order of the Grand Master, transmitted to the Grand Lodge as soon as possible. A ballot being cast on the occasion, it was unanimously agreed in the affirmative. 1769. Oct. 4.—It was agreed that the lodge should be removed to a private room at Mr. Lush's, in High Street (39 members of the lodge present). 1771. February 6.—Thomas Hodding, of Salisbury, was made a Mason. 1771. March. 20.—It was agreed that "four

new jewels should be purchased for the Treasurer, Senior W., J.W., and Secretary." 1771. May 1.—The attendance of the Salisbury Brethren was "requested to constitute a lodge the 8th of May, at Blandford, at ten o'clock in the morning."

"1771. May 15.—Visitor present, Brother Foster Knight, Esq., E.W. of Blandford Lodge."

"1771. July 17.—Two visitors from Devizes/' 1771. October 16.—A letter was read from the Grand Lodge enjoining "not to admit the following brethren as members, or otherwise, viz.: Brothers Anthony Ten Brocke, late Master; B. P. de la Coote, S.W.; John Vestenburg, J. W.; and J. Vierd, Secretary of the Caledonian Lodge, No. 263; as they were expelled the Society for having in an unjust manner traduced the Grand Lodge." 1771. December 27.—There were present at the installation of the W. M. John Lavington 38 members of the lodge and 15 visitors.

"1773. February 3.—It was agreed, *nem. con.*, that' Brother Alexander's second son should be put to school to Brother Burbidge at the expense of the lodge."

"1773. June 24.—Eelief given to a brother, a German, 2s. 6d." 1773. August 18.—A member of the lodge at Devizes, Win. Harris, petitioned for relief. 1773. November 24.—(25 brethren present). 1773. December 27.—A pair of candlesticks were presented by Brother Eobert Cooper. 1774. March 2.—A letter was read from the Grand Lodge, asking for a subscription towards building a hall. 1774. June 24.—(29 members present).

"1774. July 17.—Visitor from Devizes. "

"1774. September 7.—Visitor from Bradford." "1774. November 2.—Mr. Wm. Lush made a Mason." "1774. December 27.—John Hodding made a Mason."

"1775. January 11.—Eesolved 'That no song but what is or may be proper to be inserted in the Constitution Book shall be sung in the lodge.'" 1775. May 17.—A motion was made by Brother' Courtney, and with the unanimous con-

sent of the lodge, humbly requesting that Brother Cooper would accept the office of Provincial Master for this county, and that application be made to the Grand Lodge to obtain a deputation for that purpose. Brother Cooper at a subsequent lodge declined the honour.

"1775. December 27.—Mr. Michael Burfough received the first and second degrees of Masonry."

"1776. February 7.—Brother Burrough 'was raised to the degree of M.M. '"

"1776. August 26.—At a committee this day held to consider of an application from the Grand Lodge for a contribution towards the building and furnishing their new hall, and also for an account of registering fees and subscriptions since October, 1768, to the intent that a part thereof may be appropriated to the use of the Grand Lodge, the following reply was agreed to:—

"' That the members of the Salisbury Lodge have always entertained the warmest sense of duty and respect for their brethren of the Grand Lodge, and have cheerfully assisted to the utmost of their abilities in promoting every undertaking that was calculated for the honour of Masonry, or the benefit of any deserving brother.

""That their attention has for some years past been employed in establishing this lodge upon a permanent and respectable foundation; in the prosecution of which design they have been obliged to build and furnish a new room, from their own stock only; and that the expenses attending their endeavours have been such as they presume would have justified an application to the Grand Lodge for assistance, had they not imagined that applications for such purposes were injurious to the honour and credit of true Masonry.

"'That the burthen of their expenses has been much increased by the assistance given to the necessitous brethren of their own lodge, and to their descendants; and that the members found it necessary to pay double subscriptions for a considerable time to defray these expenses and support the reputation of their lodge.

"' That a requisition for the country lodges to provide either wholly, or in part, a hall or furniture for the brethren of the Grand Lodge, is not in our opinion consistent with the dignity of that worshipful body; and that the conveying such requisition in form of a *demand,* by annexing *penalties* to a noncompliance, has a tendency to lessen that respect which has hitherto been paid them as the *guardians* of Masonic rights and privileges.

"' That for these reasons the brethren should hold themselves excusable in declining to comply with the request of the Grand Lodge; but it is recommended that the same annual contribution which has hitherto been sent towards the General Fund of Charity should be continued this and every future year.

"' That it is with great concern this committee observes an interruption given to *the freedom* of their brethren in general by a demand of entries of the registering fees and subscriptions of each lodge, that a part thereof may be applied to the use of the Grand Lodge; under the penalties of being censured by that assembly and being deprived of the privileges of its favour and protection.

"'That the sums received in this lodge are but little more than adequate to an expense regulated by the strictest prudence and frugality; and that as the brethren have made themselves accountable for all deficiencies whenever the receipts have fallen short, we cannot consent that any surplus money be applied to the benefit of any other lodges unless on charitable or other such particular occasions.

"'That we apprehend (with all due deference to the judgment of better-informed brethren) that while we persevere in a strict attention to the constitutions and laws of Masonry, as planned by our immortal founder, and acknowledged by the fraternity through preceding ages, we cannot forfeit the esteem of any of our brethren.

"' That it has been our constant practice to act agreeable to those constitutions, and we are ready, on every just occasion, to testify our obedience to the Grand Lodge; but we can by no means assent to the payment of a tax which we consider as totally repugnant to the principles of Freemasonry, and reflecting no honour on those who either impose or suffer it.'"

'-' 1776. Sept. 4.—The Eeport of the Committee having been read, and the sense of the members present taken thereupon, it was resolved that the said Eeport is agreeable to the opinion of the brethren of this lodge, and that a copy of the same should be transcribed by the Secretary, and by him transmitted to the Grand Lodge." 1776. Oct. 16.—A letter received from Brother Haseltine, Secretary of the Grand Lodge, since last meeting, and recommending a repeal of the resolutions of Sept. 4th, was laid before the lodge, when it was unanimously resolved that the said resolutions are agreeable to the sentiments of this lodge, and were formed with the regularity usual on such occasions. That the Secretary be desired to return thanks to Brother Haseltine for his good intentions, and to inform him that as nothing has since happened to occasion a change of sentiment, it is the request of this lodge that he should lay the said resolutions before the Grand Lodge at the next quarterly communication.

"March 13. 1777.—At an extra lodge held this day in consequence of summonses from ye E.W.M., the B.W.M. informed the brethren that he had convened them for ye purpose of taking into consideration an act of the Grand Lodge at their last quarterly convention, held Feb. 5th, 1777, when they had thought proper to erase the Salisbury Lodge from their list, for having refused to comply with those requisitions, which the Salisbury Lodge thought inconsistent with the principle of P. and A.M.

" The refusal of this lodge, as contained in their memorial, dated Sept. 4th, 1777, was then read, and the opinion of the brethren being taken, it was resolved by a majority of 20 to 8 that a letter be sent to ye Secretary of the Grand Lodge, in order that the circumstances of our erasure may be reconsidered by the Grand Lodge, who, on such consideration, might possibly find it prudent to reinstate us.

"Such a step appeared the more necessary to be taken, as the members of this lodge might hereafter have occasion to appeal to the opinion of their brethren at large, when their conduct would be more justifiable, from their having endeavoured by every honourable means to preserve an union with the Grand Lodge.

"In justice to those eight brethren who were in the minority on the above question, it should be remembered that their dissenting was not founded on any desire to comply with the requisitions of ye Grand Lodge (for in this respect the brethren were unanimous), but they conceived that the affront given to so respectable a body as the Salisbury Lodge was such as rendered it beneath our attention to make any application to them whatever, and that we should be justified in an immediate appeal to the lodges at large."

"March 19. 1777.—The following letter was unanimously approved of to be transmitted to the Secretary of the Grand Lodge:—

"Eight Worshipful Sir,

"The erasure of the Salisbury Lodge, in consequence of their refusal to comply with the requisitions of the Grand Lodge, was this evening made known to the brethren at a summoned meeting; and I am directed to inform you (that it may by your means be transmitted to the Grand Lodge) that our refusal has arisen from a strict obedience to the laws, principles, and constitutions of Free and Accepted Masonry; which expressly say 'that though the Grand Lodge have an inherent power and authority to make new regulations, "See Art. 14, page 281, Brother J. Entick's "Revisal," &o., of Brother J. Anderson's ' Constitutions,' vulgar year of Masonry, 5756." the real benefit of this ancient fraternity shall in all cases be consulted, and the old landmarks carefully preserved.'

"By the late attempt of the Grand Lodge to impose a tax on the brethren at large, under penalty of erasing them from that list wherein they have a right to stand enrolled, as long as they shall preserve the principles of that constitution, the bounds prescribed by these landmarks seem to have been exceeded; the Grand Lodge has taken upon itself the exercise of a power hitherto unknown, the ancient rules of the fraternity (which gave freedom to every Mason) have been broke in upon, and that decency of submission, which is produced by an equitable government, has been changed to an extensive and, we apprehend, a justifiable resistance to the endeavours of the Grand Lodge.

"Previous, however, to any public appeal, which the members of the Salisbury Lodge may think it necessary to make to the fraternity at large, it is their desire that the requisition and refusal may again be taken into consideration, as the erasure may have been more hasty than the circumstances required; and on a second examination the Salisbury Lodge may probably be reinstated.

"I beg the favour of you to transmit an answer as soon as possible, and am

"Yours affectionately,

"john Edgak, Jun., Secretary."

"After which a motion was made and unanimously agreed to, that a copy of the above letter be sent to Brother Thos. Dunckerley, Esq., Provincial G.M. for Essex, enclosed in a letter of thanks to him for his affectionate attention to the welfare of the Salisbury Lodge at the quarterly committee, when they undeservedly were erased from the list, for that glorious struggle which ought to render them doubly respectable in the esteem of all real Masons."

The following is a copy of the letter sent to Brother Dunckerley:—

"Eight Worshipful Sir,

"Inclosed you will receive the copy of a letter which has been sent to the Worshipful Secretary of the Grand Lodge of Free and Accepted Masons (touching their erasure of the Salisbury Lodge from their list) to be by him presented at their next quarterly convention, and which by the unanimous voice of the Salisbury Lodge I was directed to lay before you, together with an assurance of the grateful sense they entertain of your affectionate regard for their welfare, and the good opinion you hold to-

wards their general conduct.

"We cannot but flatter ourselves with the hopes of your approbation when you consider the motives which influence us to action in the important, interesting, and glorious struggle with the Grand Lodge; important and interesting, as it affects the fundamental laws of our ancient fraternity; and glorious to us, as we have no other object in view than the preservation of unsullied freedom.

"As no body of men can have a greater veneration for a decent submission to superior power, so, on the other hand, whenever injustice or oppression marks the conduct of the Grand Lodge, they will always find us united and steadily resolute to oppose them.

"Thus influenced, we stand forth at once the warm partisans of legal government, and firm adversaries to every species of tyranny; and though modesty becomes the wisest in forming opinions, yet the respectability of that authority on which we ground our actions and opinions (no less than 'the laws of this ancient and noble fraternity, too sacred to be mutilated or destroyed by innovations foreign to ye good of the craft), is such as leaves us not the least occasion for doubt, but fixes in us a steady determination to persevere; and we cannot but flatter ourselves that the sera is not far off when we shall be esteemed as the saviours of Masonic freedom, against the designs of a most formidable party, who were resolved to raise their importance and splendour on the ruins of one of the most-to-be-esteemed pillars of this happy constitution.

"I am, Eight Worshipful Sir,

"With respect,

"Yours affectionately,

"john Edgar, *Jim.*

"Salisbury, *March 2Ut,* 1777.

"To Thos. Dunokerley, Esq."

"May 21, 1777.—The lodge was this evening opened in due form, and the first and second lectures worked according to order.

"The following answer to be sent to Brother Dunckerley's proposition was read and approved:—

"Sir,

"Yours, with friendly assurances to-

wards the Salisbury Lodge and generous proffers of services as a mediator between them and the Grand Lodge, I received in due time; but postponed sending you an answer till I had laid it before my brethren at their subsequent meeting, which has been done. They are sensible of the obligation done them by your affectionate zeal and kind interposition, but at the same time are too well convinced of the rectitude of their proceedings to think of retracting any of their resolutions respecting the demand made by the Grand Lodge.

"Warm with these sentiments, they wait resigned the issue of your application on their behalf, and sincerely join in wishes for your temporal and eternal welfare, "Iam, "Your obliged and very humble Servant, "John Edgab, Jun. "Salisbury, May 16th, 1777." 1777. June 4.—Brother Michael Burrough was appointed Secretary.

1777. July 16.—A request was received from the new lodge at Eingwood for a copy of the bye-laws.

"1777. Aug. 6.—At the lodge held this evening the brethren then present agreed that the letter hereunder copied shall be sent to Brother Dunckerley, in order to be sent to the Grand Lodge:—

"We, the officers of a late lodge held at Salisbury, and having been appointed to settle and determine a dispute between the Grand Lodge and that Society of which we have been nominated the representatives, humbly beg leave to represent to the Grand Lodge, that by reason of the engagements of the Salisbury Brethren in building their own lodge, and relieving the necessities of their distressed members, &c., they have not had an opportunity of attending duly to the requisitions of the Grand Lodge for a remittance of five shillings for each new-made member, and therefore have neglected to receive that sum from such as have been admitted from Oct. 29th, 1768, to this day, many of whom are i now far distant from Salisbury. They are sorry that for this neglect they have incurred the censure of the Grand Lodge, and have directed us to inform the members of that Eight Worshipful Body that it is their earnest wish to preserve their favour and protection, and that they humbly hope a due attention in future to the payment of the said sum of five shillings for every person hereafter admitted will be accepted as a sufficient proof of their loyalty and obedience, so as to induce the Grand Lodge to reinstate them as before the commencement of the present controversy.

"H. Skeats, W.M. Geo. Webb.

John Webb, P.M. Fras. Shuttleworth.

Jos. Hodgson, S.W. Wm. Burbidge,

John Edgar, Jun., J.W. Geo. Scandover.

Alex. Minty. Alex. Martin.

Wm. Lush. Ben. Steedman.

'Jas. Walker. Wm. Weeks.

Henry Short. Michl. Burrough, Sec.

"Michael Burrough, Sec.

"N.B.—Notwithstanding the compliance of this lodge with the demand of five shillings for every person hereafter to be made a Mason therein, it must be observed that the legality of this demand was still denied; but the brethren taking into consideration the evils that might arise from their causing any division in Masonry (more especially as the Grand Lodge had given up every other part of their requisition), it was thought most prudent to acquiesce in this point. "

"Motion was made and unanimously agreed to that the resolutions of the Grand Lodgo shall be entered in the bye-laws respecting the impropriety of Free and Accepted Masons countenancing those who call themselves Ancient Masons."

"1777. August 30.—At an extra lodge held this evening the W.M. gave in a letter from Brother Dunckerley signifying his intention of visiting this lodge on the happy occasion of its re-union with the Grand Lodge, and likewise at the same time informing the brethren that the Most Worshipful Lord Charles Montague would hold a Provincial Grand Lodge on Tuesday, 2nd of Sept., at the sign of the Half Moon in Southampton, where his lordship would he glad to see all or any of the brethren of the Salisbury Lodge at nine o'clock in the forenoon in order to go in procession to church."

"1777. Sept. 2.—The brethren attended (as visitors) a Provincial Grand Lodge for Hampshire, held at the Star Inn, Southampton, when all the members went in open lodge to Holy Eood Church, and heard an eloquent and learned discourse from the Eev. Brother Scott. The collection at the church-door amounted to £20 16s. 4d., which was distributed the next day to poor housekeepers in Southampton not receiving parochial alms. The sermon being ended, an anthem on the occasion was sung by Brother Gundry, and the brethren then returned to the Star, whence they adjourned to dinner at the Half Moon.

"The whole proceedings of the day were conducted with the greatest regularity, and could not fail of impressing on the minds of the public a memorable idea of the happy effects of those institutions which have virtue for their foundation, and all the mild affections of the soul for the ornaments of their superstructure." 1777. Sept. 15. A letter from Brother Dunckerley appointing Monday, 23rd inst., for holding a Provincial Grand Lodge was read, and the necessary measures for the conduct of that day were agreed upon.

"Eesolved that £3 3s. should be given to the P.G.M. towards the Fund of Charity."

"1777. Sept. 22.—For 7 dozen of plain Masons' glasses, £1 11s. 6d."

"1777. Sept. 22.—Cash received of Brothers Hodgson and "Weeks for tickets sold at the dinner of the Provincial Grand Lodge, £12."

Mem.: The minute-book from 1777 to 1794 is missing, whilst the account-book is extant.

£ s. d.

"1777.—By bill for 1 dozen of wax lights and carriage 118 8.

"1779. Oct. 6.—To Brother Dunckerley's son, in distress 0 10 6

"1780. April 6.—Brother Crabb's biU for silver labels to the Master and S. W. Chairs 2 6 6

"1782. Jan. 29.—Expenses attending a petition to the Grand Lodge....076

"1783. March 8.—By carriage of Petition to the Grand Lodge 0 10

"1783. June 26.—By carrying Forte Piano 0 10

"1784. Feb. 14.—By subscription towards the relief of the poor of this city during the inclemency of the season.... 10 10 0

"1785. May 7.—Cost for apprenticing Brother Minty's son 5 5 0

"1785. June 26.—For cutting the Masons' arms in paper 0 5 0

"1789. Jan. 21.—Relief of the poor.. 21 0 0

"1790. March 16.—Printing 1,000 sum-£ s. d.

monses.14 0

"1794. Aug. 3.—By county subscription.626

Mem.: The minute-book recommences in 1794..

"1794. Dec. 27.—Present 42 brethren and 3 visitors."

"1795. Dec. 27.—The W.P.M. Brother Burbidge recommended Brother Wyndham as Provincial Grand Master of Wilts."

"1796. June 8.—Eesolved that in future the expenses of making should be raised from £3 10s. 6d. to £4 11s. 6d. ; that is to say, £4 4s. for the use of the lodge, 5s. to the Grand Hall, 2s. 6d. to the Grand Secretary; and that the charges of raising a brother to the degree of Master Mason should be £1 11s. 6d. Subscriptions to be raised to 10s. per quarter." 1799. July 17.—In a letter in reply respecting the initiation of a brother in the Sarum Lodge occurs the number of the lodge, viz. "the undermentioned being master and wardens of the Sarum Lodge, No. 34." 1800. Jan. 15.— The following letter received from the Grand Lodge was read:—

"Grand Lodge, *20th Nov.,* 1799.

"The Grand Lodge having appointed a committee to examine how far the resolution of the Grand Lodge of 7th February, 1798, directing two shillings per annum to be paid by every member of a lodge towards liquidating the debts of the Society has been complied with, and to inquire what further may be requisite to give due effect to the said resolution; and it appearing that several lodges had neglected to conform thereto, the committee, on mature deliberation, were unanimously of opinion, that it is of the utmost importance to the welfare of the Society that the said regulation should be punctually observed, and for that purpose recommend to the Grand Lodge to adopt the following resolutions:—

" ' That every lodge has full power over its members to enforce the laws of the Grand Lodge, and that on non-compliance therewith by any of its members, it is the duty of the lodge to expel such member or members, the Grand Lodge in respect of this law considering the lodge as answerable.

' '' That notice be given to such lodges as have not complied with the above-mentioned law, that unless they make their payments in conformity thereto on or before the Grand Lodge to be held on the 12th February next, the lodges in default shall be considered as in contempt, and be erased from the lists of lodges.'

"The foregoing resolutions were adopted by the Grand Lodge and ordered accordingly. The lodges are therefore enjoined to conform thereto, and it behoves every lodge to be particularly careful not to incur a forfeiture of its constitution at the present period, as no fresh constitution can be granted.

"william White, G.S.

"This lodge having likewise maturely deliberated on the above resolutions do unanimously resolve *not* to conform to the said resolutions.

"This lodge unanimously agreed to write to the Grand Lodge respecting the letter received from the Grand Secretary respecting the payment of two shillings per annum from each member, and to inform them that from the particular state of the funds of the lodge, it was out of their power to agree to their request.

"Burbidge, E.W.M. Webb.

"1800. Nov. 19.—At a summoned lodge held this evening, the first and second lectures were worked according to order.

"Agreeable to the report of the committee and the determination of the last lodge, the brethren were summoned accordingly, to take into consideration the requisition from the Grand Lodge of

two shillings per annum from each brother towards the Liquidation Fund.

"The question having been Masonically put, the brethren proceeded to ballot, and to the honour of the Sarum Lodge, they unanimously agreed *not* to contribute to this requisition.

"Ordered that the Master do communicate the same to the Grand Secretary.

"The W.P.M. recommended a proposal for forming a Grand Lodge in Salisbury, independent of the Grand Lodge of England

"That it should be debated in the several lodges at their respective meetings, whether (the Grand Lodge having thought proper to erase them from their list) it be expedient to form such an independent Grand Lodge; and if it be resolved in the affirmative, a committee, consisting of throe members of each lodge, should bo appointed to meet on some early day to take the same into consideration, and to form a plan for the establishment of it; as soon as convenient after their decision a general meeting or convocation of all the subscribing members of each lodge should be convened by them to receive the report of the committee and determine thereon.

"The above resolution was unanimously agreed to, and Brother Maton, Brother Hodding, and Brother Burbidge, Sen., were appointed a committee for the Sarum Lodge. The officers of the different lodges attended, viz. Brother Trycke, Brother Burrough, Brother Weeks, Brother Hodding, Jun., Brother Lane, Brother Eead, Brother Jeboult, Brother "Willmot, and approved of the above said resolution, and agreed to communicate with their respective lodges accordingly."

"1801. March 14.—The Worshipful Wardens proposed that some artist be employed to paint a proper design to be used at makings and raisings." 1801. June 3.—A letter was received from Brother Henry James, of Berkeley, Gloucestershire, Provincial Grand Master for Bristol.

"1802. Jan. 6.—Eesolved that in consequence of the erasure by the Grand Lodge of the Sarum Lodge from their list, a proposal for forming a Grand

Lodge in Salisbury, independent of the Grand Lodge of England, should be debated in the several lodges." 1802. Dec. 27.—Three brethren, members of the Lodge of Peace and Concord, Isle of Wight, were raised to the degree of M. M.

1807. Jan. 21.—The lodge appears to have fallen to ten or a dozen since the dispute with Grand Lodge.

"1809. Oct. 18.—It was unanimously agreed that this lodge, in conjunction with the Lodge Apollo, meet on the 28th of this month, to walk in procession to the Cathedral Church, on the occasion of his Majesty's accession to the fiftieth year of his reign, and that the following brethren compose a committee for the arrangement thereof, to meet at ten o'clock on Thursday, October 19th, 1809:—

Committee.

Brother Burbidge, E.W.M.

Sutton, W.P.M.

Blown, W.S.W.

Morris, W.J.W.

Jeboult, of the Apollo Lodge.

Rhoades,,, ,,

Elderton, of the Sarum Lodge.

Boles, ,,,,

"The above committee, having met as agreed upon, came to the resolution 'that the Sarum and Apollo Lodges dine together on the anniversary of his Majesty's accession, and that an advertisement appear in the *Salisbury Journal,* requesting the attendance of the neighbouring lodges and all other brethren to join in the procession.'"

"1809. Oct. 25.—The Sarum and Apollo Lodges assembled this morning, and, joined by various other brethren, went in procession to the Market Place to attend the Corporation, and from thence to the Cathedral in the following order:—

Tyler, with a drawn sword.

Two Stewards, with badge of office and wands.

Junior Brethren, two and two.

A Lewis, carrying a column.

Two Junior Wardens, with badge of office and wands.

Two Lewises, bearing two columns.

Two Senior Wardens, with badge of

office and wands.

Two Secretaries, with rolls, badge of office, and wands.

Two Treasurers, with badge of office.

Three Lewises, bearing the three lights.

The Lodge, borne by four Lewises.

A Lewis, bearing the constitution.

The Chaplain.

A Lewis, bearing a perfect ashler.

Two Masters, with jewels and wands.

Two Past Masters, with jewels and wands.

Senior Members, two and two.

Two Stewards, with badge of office and wands.

Tyler, with a drawn sword.

"The procession having returned in the same order, after attending the Corporation to the Council Chamber returned to the lodge, where the Eev. Brother Harrington, the Chaplain of the lodge, delivered a most impressive and appropriate address to the brethren, who afterwards dined together." EXTRACTS FEOM THE MINUTE-BOOKS OF LODGE ELIAS DE DEEHAM, SALISBUEY.

1851. Feb. 11.—At a preliminary meeting for organizing the lodge, it was reported "that the petition for a Warrant, supported by the Eoyal Gloucester Lodge, No. 152, at Southampton, had been presented to the G.M., and that the Warrant had been granted." 1851. March 11.—The petition for a Warrant was read, in which it was stated that "the Lodge was called Elias de Derham after the Principal and Superintendent of the works of the Cathedral at Sarum for nearly twenty years." The Warrant was also read. 1851. April 8.—Henry James Fowle Swayne, Esq., of the Island, Wilton, was balloted for, unanimously elected, and initiated. 1853. Feb. 9.—Visitor: Brother Deacon, Provincial Grand Master for Hampshire. 1867. Sept. 5.—It was agreed to change quarters from the White Hart Hotel to the Temperance Hall, which was to be rented.

"1869. March 4.—A communication from the Grand Secretary was read, stating that "the Most Worshipful the Grand Master has fixed 14th April for the inauguration of the new building in Great Queen Street, London, and desires the appointment of a steward to attend from this lodge." 1873. Sept. 11. —A report of the visit of the children and instructors of the Masonic Schools to Salisbury and Stonehenge on 8th August, and of their entertainment by Brother Horatio Ward and this lodge, was directed to be entered upon the minutes.

1874. Nov. 6.—The Proyincial Grand Lodge was received by this lodge. 1878. March 14.—The report and decision of the Grand Lodge, with regard to the Grand Orient of France, was read. 1878. Nov. 14.—A building fund was agreed to be raised by the investment of the balance of the funds of the lodge at the end of each year. LIST OF WOKSHIPFUL MASTEES OF THE SALISBURY LODGE,

Tear.	Worshipful Master.
1732.	
1733.	
1734.	
1735.	
1736.	
1737.	
1738.	
1739.	
1740.	
1741.	
1742.	
1743. 1744.	
1745.	
1746.	
1747.	
1748.	
1749.	
1750.	
1751.	
1752.	
1753.	
1754.	
1755.	
1756.	
1757.	
1758.	
1759.	
1760.	
1761.	

Worshipful Master.

James Drake

Joseph Mede

Charles Blake

James Case

(John Burrough, Deputy W

George Baily.

John Lightbody

Thomas Brown

John Corfe

George Baily.

Francis Jarrett

George Baily.

Thomas Brown

William Potts.

John Staples.

»»»

Thomas Morris

John Kenworthy

James Morris.

Thomas Mitchell

George Burbidge

William Southwell

William Pride.

John Knight.

John Cowell.

William Pride.

John Edgar

Ambrose Courtney

Thomas Brown

Joshua Mabberley

John Edgar

LIST OF WORSHIPFUL MASTERS OF LODGE ELIAS DE DERHAM.

No. of Meetings

Year. Worshipfol Master. of the Lodge.

1851. Thomas Richard Moore, M.D.. 12 1852. James Smith 7 1853. Philip Pinckney Cother... 7 1854. ,, ,,... 7 1855. 5 1856. James Brown...... 2 1857. William Wadham Young.. 7 1858. Pvohert Stokes...... 7 1859. Beverley Robinson. ... 6 1860. William Dore 2 1861. John Major Cardell.... 9 1862. ,,.... 7 1863. Rev. Edward H. Elers... 8 '1864. Frederick King.... 9 1865. Charles Wadham Wyndham.. 8 1866. Edmund George Benson... 8 1867. Richard Stowell Bryan... 8 1868. Frederick King....11 1869. Dr. Humphrey Purnell Blackmore. 15 1870. Horatio Ward 7 1871. ,, ,, 15 1872. E. Henry Taylor.... 8 1873. Frederick Griffin.... 8 1874. P. H. Perman 13 1875. W. G. Stodart 12 1876. John Rumbold 12 1877. Francis S. Russell.... 10 1878. Thomas Norwood.... 10 1879. A. Tucker 10 TURK'S HEAD LODGE.

It has not yet been ascertained what the

Turk's Head Lodge had to do with Salisbury, but we find that where the entries in the minute-book and ledger of the Turk's Head Lodge leave off those of the Salisbury Lodge commence, and were continued until the books were filled up. Still, as they throw light upon Masonic doings of a century and a half ago, it has been thought advisable to insert a few extracts from the books of that lodge.

EXTEACTS FEOM THE MINUTE-BOOKS OF TURK'S HEAD LODGE.

"1738. Feb. 27.—Minutes of a private convention of the Turk's Head Lodge:—

"That the Master, Wardens, and brethren of the lodge held at Dale's Coffee House, in Warwick Street, near Golden Square, having regularly removed their lodge to the Turk's Head Tavern in Greek Street, Soho, the W. M. Edward Hody thought it necessary to summon the brethren to go through the accounts, and take a list of the members.

"Lodge opened—Samuel Smith, S. W., and Philip Parry Hetherington, J. W. John Chalmers was elected Secretary, and it was agreed that a silver jewel should be purchased for his use, 'and his health was drunk with the usual ceremony;' afterwards the lodge was regularly closed with the songs of the craft, at half an hour past eleven o'clock."

K

"1738. March 16.—Ee-election of Dr. Hody as W.M.; his health was drunk; and the lodge was closed with songs, and with the usual ceremony of the craft."

"1738. April 20.—An examination was passed in Masonry by the Master and "Wardens. The Secretary of the lodge held at the Talbot Head, Channel Eow, requested, in the name of the Master and brethren of this lodge, the favour of the laws of this lodge, in order to transcribe them for the better regulation of their lodge."

"1738. May 18.—A brother having been balloted for, elected, and 'instituted,' the laws and penalties thereto annexed were read by the Secretary this appears to have been done at each 'in-stitution' of a brother. It was agreed that the names and places of abode of all present, and in future of all new members, be immediately given to the landlord, 'in order to have them properly summoned.'"

"1738. June 23.—It was agreed that the lodge should lend the laws and books of the lodge to be copied by the Secretaries of the lodges at the Key and Garter in Pall Mall, and Law's Coffee House."

"1738. July 20.—It was unanimously agreed that 'a book should be provided at the expense of the lodge, wherein to insert the lectures that should be read in this lodge (with the consent of the lecturer) for the perusal of the brethren of this lodge.' Proposed and agreed to, *nem. eon.*, 'that the new Constitution Book should be subscribed for.'"

"1738. Aug. 17.—Three 'musicians' were initiated, but excused 'admission fee,' in consideration of the agreeable entertainment which we shall receive from such brethren." 1738. Sept 21.—Eeference was made to this lodge "previous to its removal in 1735," and that Brother Adams was then the W.M. 1738. Oct. 19.—It was agreed that as fault was found with the wine, '' a pipe of good wine should be fixed upon by some of the brethren, and that upon their approbation the whole should be bottled off, and the Masons' seal placed on each bottle, and kept for the use of the lodge only." The committee appointed for the purpose consisted of:—
The Master And His Two Wardens.
Brother Bishop. Brother Pelatan.
Brother Winkles. Brother Porter.
Brother Adams. Brother Tristram.
1738. Nov. 16.—A bye-law was agreed to that "as often as it shall be thought proper that this lodge have a full clothing, it shall be on the feast day of our patron, St. John the Evangelist." 1738. Dec. 20.—"A private convention" for an initiation was held. 1738. Dec. 21.—Brother Hetherington was called upon by the Master for his lecture, but excused himself on account of business preventing him, but promised it on the next lodge night, or the voluntary forfeiture of a gallon of wine.

"1739. Feb. 15.—Ordered that this lodge be clothed with aprons only, good, large, and glazed, at 14d. per piece, at the next lodge night. Ordered that at the next general clothing every brother shall write his name upon his apron, and that they may be committed to the care of the Tyler, who shall deliver each brother his own apron on every lodge night, before he enters the lodge, and at no other time whatever."

"1739. March 15.—Ordered that our Brother Delarant (the proprietor of the tavern), the Tyler, and the Drawer, have aprons at the expense of this lodge. Ee-election of Dr. Hody, after which the lodge was closed at high twelve."

"1739. Aug. 16.—Part of the Book of Constitutions was read by the Secretary. Brother Mills having been lately blessed with a lewis, was pleased to present this lodge with a crown bowl of punch upon that happy occasion, and the young lewis's health was drunk to in form."

"1739. Sept. 20.—Our Brother Delarant presented the lodge with a bowl of punch on his having a lewisa born, and her health was drunk in form."

"1739. Dec. 20.—Brother Goodchild desiring the lend of our laws for the lodge at the Ax and Gate, Westminster, it was readily granted. It was ordered that the laws of this lodge be copied by the Secretary for the use of the Eev. Dean Bruce, our brother."

"1739. January 17.—Our Brother Francis Burton did this night entertain the lodge with an agreeable lecture on Architectural Proportions, for which thanks were returned to him, and his health was drunk in due form. Agreed by the members of this lodge to meet here on the 25th of February in order to dine."

Here the Minute Book suddenly ceases, except that on the next page, in quite a different handwriting, appears as follows:—

"At a lodge held the 27th December, 1766, being tho anniversary of St. John the Evangelist, Brother Bobt. Cooper was installed Master and chose his officers."

Thenfollow alist of officers, including Brother Staples, Treasurer, and a list of members, all of them being Salisbury men.

End of Booh.

On the reverse side of the book are the accounts for 1768 to 1771, headed:—

"Three Swans, Salisbury Lodge, No. . Accountbook from St. John's Day, in June, 5768;" and they commence with " arrears depending from old book."

LANSDOWNE LODGE OF UNITY, No. 626.

Warrant Dated December 7th, 1853. Meets At The New Hall, Chippenham. Lodges Held On The Second Tuesday In Each Month, At 5 P.m.

Installation Of The W.M. In December.

Number or Members Of The Lodge, 45, Of Whom 7 ARE P-.M.

LANSDOWNE LODGE OF UNITY.

This lodge was founded immediately upon the appointment of Lord Methuen as Provincial Grand Master, in 1853, and he installed his Deputy Provincial Grand Master as its first W.M.

The lodge carried on its duties at Calne for a time, but the numbers of the brethren fell off, and it was only by one or two of them (including the highly esteemed Treasurer, Brother Lane) very generously keeping up the subscriptions, to the Grand Lodge and Provincial Grand Lodge, and other necessary payments, that a forfeiture of the Warrant was avoided.

In 1869 the D.P.G.M., Sir Daniel Gooch, Bart.", M.P., having been appointed P.G.M. for Berks and Bucks, and it having been arranged for the Methuen Lodge to accompany him to that Province, he, as a graceful leavetaking, made use of his great influence and popularity to successfully resuscitate the Lansdowne Lodge and re-establish it at Chippenham, where the numbers have steadily increased until it has become one of the strongest lodges in the Province.

The present Deputy Provincial Grand Master, Sir Gabriel Goldney, Bart., M.P., and Worshipful Brother Alderman Eobert Nicholas Fowler, M.P., have filled the chair of the lodge, and contin-

ue to take great interest in its welfare.

A HISTORY OF FREEMASONRY, ETC. 137 EXTEACTS FBOM THE MINUTE-BOOKS OF LANSDOWNE LODGE OF UNITY. 1854. Jan. 17.—A meeting was held at the Town Hall, Calne. Present:— Lord Methuen, P.G.M.; D. Gooch, D. P.G.M.; Provincial Grand Officers, Brethren, and Visitors, upon the occasion of the installation of "Worshipful Brother Daniel Gooch as W.M. 1854. Oct. 4.—Brother Henry Alworth Merewether was elected as a joining member of this lodge. 1855. Nov. 5. —William Henry Poynder, Esq., of Hartham Park, was initiated. 1860. Feb. 8.—A proposal was carried unanimously that steps should be taken to obtain the sanction of the Grand Lodge for the meeting of this lodge alternately at the Lansdowne Arms Hotel, Calne, and the Angel Hotel, Chippenham. 1868. Dec. 23.—The number of this lodge upon the Eegister of the Grand Lodge changed from 909 to 626. 1869. June 8.—A resolution was carried unanimously that the meetings should in future be held at Chippenham. 1869. July 13.—Brother Gabriel Goldney, M.P., was elected as a joining member. 1870. Jan. 6.—Brother Eobert Nicholas Fowler, M.P., was elected as a joining member. 1871. June 21. The death of Brother Francis Stewart Wilmot, the Senior Warden of the lodge, was reported, and a vote of condolence with his widow was unanimously passed. 1872. Feb. 13. It was unanimously agreed that addresses of congratulation on the happy restoration to health of H.E.H. the Prince of Wales should be drawn up, and presented to her Majesty and his Eoyal Highness through the proper channel. 1872. March 20. The Provincial Grand Lodge was received by this lodge. 1872. August 2. The death of Brother Eev. W. M. P. Pym, Chaplain of the Lodge and Grand Chaplain of the Province, was reported, and the Secretary was directed to convey to the widow the deep feelings of regret entertained by the lodge upon the death of so estimable a Mason, and their sympathy with her in her sad loss. 1873. June 10. The Bye-laws as amended were passed and adopted, and

the Secretary was directed to forward them to the Provincial Grand Master for his approval and confirmation. 1873. Aug. 4. Brother G. Goldney, M.P., was installed Master of the lodge in the presence of a large number of Past Masters and brethren from this and the neighbouring Provinces. 1874. Aug. 31. A resolution was unanimously passed to convey the very cordial thanks of the lodge to Brother G. Goldney, M.P., the V.W. Deputy Provincial Grand Master, for the manner in which he had filled the office as Master of the lodge during the past year. 1875. May 11. Brother F. H. Goldney reported that he, as the W. M. of the lodge, together with his S.W. and J.W., several P.M.'s, and the Secretary, had attended the Grand Lodge held in the Albert Hall, Kensington, on the occasion of the installation of H.E. H. the Prince of Wales as Grand Master of England. 1876. August 30. Installation of Brother E. N. Fowler, M.P., as Worshipful Master by Brother G. Goldney, M.P., the Deputy Provincial Grand Master, in the presence of a large meeting of the brethren. 1877. Dec. 10. A Past Treasurer's jewel and a ring were presented to Brother Joseph Lane by the brethren of the lodge, in token of their high esteem for him, and in remembrance of his having filled the office of Treasurer of the lodge for nine years, and having so ably supported the lodge during the eighteen years he had been a member of it, and particularly during its periods of decadence and transition from Calne to Chippenham.

A Past Master's jewel, with a suitable inscription thereon, was presented to Brother E. N. Fowler, M.P., in recognition of the benefits the lodge had derived from him, particularly during his year of office as Master of the lodge.

1878. April 9. The following report from the Grand Lodge was read:—

"The committee appointed at the last Grand Lodge, on Wednesday, the 5th of December, 1877, to consider the recent action of the Grand Orient of France, beg to report that the Grand Lodge of England has received information that the Grand Orient of France has resolved by a considerable majority to rescind the 1st and 2nd paragraphs of its Constitution, and to substitute for them the following laws.

"*The laws as they formerly stood read thus:—*

"' 1. Freemasonry, an institution essentially philanthropic, philosophical, and progressive, has for its object the inquiry after truth, the study of universal morality, sciences, and arts, and the practice of universal benevolence.

'"2. Its principles are the existence of God, the immortality of the soul, and *humaine solidarity.* "' 3. It regards liberty of conscience as the common right of every man, and excludes no person on account of his belief.

"' 4. Its motto is Liberty, Equality, and Fraternity.'

"*As they now stand they are as follows:—*

"' 1. Freemasonry, an institution essentially philanthropic, philosophical, and progressive, has for its object the inquiries after truth, the study of universal morality, sciences, and arts, and the practice of benevolence.

"' 2. Its principles are absolute liberty of conscience and *humaine solidariti.* " 3. It excludes no person on account of his belief.

! 4. Its motto is Liberty, Equality, and Fraternity.'

"The committee have carefully considered this action on the part of the Grand Orient of France, and having regard to all the circumstances of the case, they have unanimously agreed to recommend the following resolutions for the adoption of Grand Lodge:—

"That this Grand Lodge views with profound regret the step taken by the Grand Orient of France, in thus removing from its Constitutions those paragraphs which assert a belief in the existence of TGAOTU, because such an alteration is opposed to the traditions, practice, and feelings of all true and genuine Masons from the earliest to the present time.

"That this Grand Lodge, whilst always anxious to receive in the most fraternal spirit the brethren of any foreign Grand Lodge whose proceedings are conducted according to the Ancient

Landmarks of the Order, of which a belief in TGAOTU is the first and most important, cannot recognise as true and genuine brethren any who have been initiated in lodges which either deny or ignore that belief.

"That in view of the foregoing Eesolution the "Worshipful Masters of all lodges holding under the Grand Lodge of England be directed not to admit any foreign brother as a visitor, unless he is duly vouched for, or unless his certificates show that ho has been initiated according to the ancient rites and ceremonies in a lodge professing belief in TGAOTU, and unless he himself shall acknowledge that this belief is an essential Landmark of the Order.

"That a copy of the foregoing.Eesolutions be transmitted to the Grand Lodges of Ireland and Scotland, to each Grand Lodge with which the Grand Lodge of England is in communication, and to the Worshipful Masters of all lodges holding under the Grand Lodge of England, and that it be an instruction to the Worshipful Master of each lodge to read these Eesolutions at the first meeting after the reception thereof, and to direct that they shall be entered upon the Minutes. London. February 22nd, 1878." 1878. June 11. The death of Brother Eev. E. 0. Eoach, Chaplain of the lodge, and Past Assistant Grand Chaplain of the Province, was reported, and a vote of condolence with his widow was passed.

The congratulations of the brethren were offered to Brother E. N. Fowler, P. P.G.P., on his being elected an Alderman of the City of London.

1879. July 8. Past Masters' jewels, with suitable inscriptions thereon, were presented by the brethren of the lodge to Brother P. H. Goldney, P.G. Treasurer, and Brother P. H. Phillips, P.A.G.D. of C, in fraternal recognition of their meritorious services to the lodge. 1879. Dec. 9. A Past Master's jewel, with suitable inscription thereon, was presented by the brethren of the lodge to Brother E. Eyres, P.P.G.P., in recognition of his services to the lodge. LIST OF WOESHIPFUL MASTERS OF LANSDOWNE LODGE OF UNITY.

No. of Meetings

Year. Worshipful Master. of the lodge.
1854. Sir Daniel Gooch, Bart., M.P.. 9
1855. Henry Weaver.... 12 1856.
Thomas Large Henly... 10 1857. John
N. Ladd.... 8 1858. William Rogers.... 3
1859. John Spencer.... 3 1860. „ 6 1861.
Joseph Burt 2 1862. „, 1 1863.
1864.
1865.
1866.
1867.
1868. Joseph Burt.... 1869. George
James Parfitt 1870. Wakefield Simpson
1871. William Thompson 1872. Edward T. Inslrip. 1873. Sir Gabriel Goldney, Bart., M.P. 1874. Frederick Hastings Goldney. 1875. B. H. Watts.... 1876.
Robert Nicholas Fowler, M.P. 1877.
Francis Henry Phillips. 1878. Edwin
Eyres.... 1879. Richard Careless 7 11 9
9 9 7 7 5 7 10 li LODGE OF CONCOED,
No. 632.

Warrant Dated April 3rd, 1854.

Meets At The Masonic Hall, Trowbridge.

Lodges Held On Tuesday Nearest The Full Moon In

Each MoNrn, At 7 P.M. Installation Of The W.M. In January. Number Of Members Of The Lodge, 44, Of Whom 9

Are P.M.

KOYAL AECH CHAPTER.

Warrant Dated May 5th, 1869.

Meets At The Masonic Hall, Trowbridge.

Chapters Held On 3rd Wednesday In January, March,

May, September, And November, At 6 P.m. Installation Of Principals In September. Number Of Members Of The Chapter, 16, Of Whom 7 Are P.Z.

LODGE OF CONCOED.

Theee was a former lodge, No. 850, which met at the Three Tuns Inn, Trowhridge, but it ceased to exist some years before the foundation of the present lodge, and the only record of it consists of rough minutes of two meetings, held on June 8th and August 28th, 1831.

The existing lodge was founded in 1854, and its number, 915, was in 1863 closed up to 632.

A HISTORY OF FREEMASONRY, ETC.
145 EXTEACTS FEOM THE MINUTE-
BOOKS OF LODGE OF CONOOED.
1854. May 16.—Consecration of the lodge and installation of the W.M. by the D.P.G.M., Brother D. Gooch. 1855. March 6.—The bye-laws proposed at the last meeting were read and confirmed. 1855. Dec. 20.—The joining fees were returned to two brethren "on account of their having been members of the former lodge, No. 850, in this town." 1858. Jan. 24.—The Provincial Grand Lodge was received by this lodge. 1860. Dec. 19.—A vote of thanks was passed to Brother E. de M. Lawson for his gift of a set of tracingboards. 1863. Sept. 29.—An announcement was read from the Grand Lodge that the number of the lodge was changed from 915 to 632. 1865. Oct. 10.—The Provincial Grand Lodge was received by this lodge. 1866. Jan. 23.—The first meeting of the lodge in the Masonic Hall. 1866. May 9.—A vote of thanks was passed to Brother E. de M. Lawson for his gift of a pair of Masonic pillars and a Master's canopy. 1868. Nov. 30. —The recommendation for a Eoyal Arch Chapter to be attached to the lodge was signed in open lodge. 1869. May 25. — Certain members of the lodge resident in Bradford-on-Avon being desirous of forming themselves into a lodge by the style of the Lodge of Friendship and Unity, No. 1271, the recommendation of their petition was signed in open lodge. 1871. Nov. 3.— The Provincial Grand Lodge was received by this lodge. 1873. Sept. 9. — Certain members of the lodge resident in Warminster being desirous of forming themselves into a lodge by the style of the Longleat Lodge, No. 1478, the recommendation of their petition was signed in open lodge. LIST OF WOESHIP-FUL MASTEES OF LODGE OF CONCOED.
Tear.
1854.
1855.
1856.
1857.
1858.
1859.
1868.

1861.
1862.
1863.
1864.
1865.
1866.
1867.
1868.
1869.
1870.
1871.
1872.
1873.
1874.
1875.
1876.
1877.
1878.
1879.

WILTSHIEE LODGE OF FIDELITY, No. 663,
Warrant Dated February 27th, 1856.
Meets At The Town Hall, Devizes.
Lodges Held On The Third Thursday In Every Month,
Except May, June, July, And August, At 7 P.m. Installation Of The W.M. In January. Number Of Members Of The Lodge, 40, Of Whom 10
Are P.M.
DEVIZES LODGES.
Masonby is of ancient date in Devizes, but unfortunately there are no particulars of the earlier lodges except references to visitors coming from one of these to the Salisbury Lodge during the years 1771 to 1773, and of that lodge it is recorded in the Grand Lodge minutes that it was in 1778 struck off the list; but we find that another one, termed the "Old Lodge," No. 270, was subsequently constituted under the authority of the "Ancient," or "Atholl," Grand Lodge (which was an independent Grand Lodge formed by seceders from the Grand Lodge of England, in 1738), and the entries of it in the minute-book run from 1792 to 1796, when a blank occurs until 1812. No explanation is given for the absence of meetings during these intervening years, but, at all events, Brother E. F. Williams continued to be W.M. from 1792 to 1797, and in 1812 he is still W.M., which office he held until his resignation of it in 1821.

Doubts, however, seem to have arisen at one time as to the propriety of such a long tenure of office, and the Grand Lodge was communicated with upon the subject, but the recommendation of the Grand Secretary (contained in the following letter) that another W.M. should be elected in the place of Brother Williams was disregarded.
A HISTORY OF FREEMASONRY, ETC.
151
London, *January 19th,* 1818. "Worshipful Sir and Brother,
"In reference to your letter of 13th inst., respecting the office of Master of your lodge, allow me to say that as the law stands it is *imperative* that no brother should continue longer in office than two years *successively*. It therefore becomes you to elect another to the chair who, if not sufficiently competent for all the duties, you might assist, or act in his stead whenever occasion requires.
"I am, Worshipful Sir,
'" Your very obedient Servant and Brother,
Edw. Harper. G.S. Mr. E. F. Williams.
The letter, dated October 12th, 1825, from the joint Grand Secretaries, W. H. White and E. Harper, to Brother J. Ellen, W.M. of the Devizes Lodge, in which they "acknowledge receipt of your letter, stating that, owing to deaths and other uncontrollable circumstances, the lodge had come to the painful determination of discontinuing the lodge," and calling attention to the laws of the Society under which it became absolutely necessary that if the lodge were dissolved the Warrant of Constitution should be delivered up to the Grand Master, heralded the coming end, for in the minute-book there is the following entry for May 5th, 1826:—
"Memorandum. Sold By Auction.
And the Treasurer's account-book shows the division of the regalia, thus:—
"E. F. Williams.. Master's & P.M. Jewels.
G. Smith
J. Neate
— Burt
J. Ellen

G. White
T. B. Smith
. S.W. Jewel.
. J.W.
Treas.
Secretary and one Mercury
One Dove and one Mercury
One Dove

This Secretary's jewel is now in the possession of Brother William Nott, the Secretary of the present Devizes Lodge, to whom it was presented by the late Brother Ellen.

"London, *Oct. 12th,* 1825.

"Sir and Brother,

"We have to acknowledge the receipt of your letter of the 12th ult., stating that, owing to death and other uncontrollable circumstances, the lodge had come to the painful determination of discontinuing the lodge.

"However we may deplore the causes which have urged you and the other brethren to adopt this measure, it becomes our duty to call your attention to the laws of the Society as contained in the Book of Constitutions, particularly Arts. 31 and 32 in p. 68, wherein it is declared that if a lodge become in arrear of its payments to the Grand Lodge for one year, or does not meet during that period, such lodge is liable to erasure, &c. And if a lodge be dissolved, the Constitution shall be delivered up to the Grand Master, and shall not on any account be transferred without his consent.

" Hence it will be obvious that it will not only be in accordance with the laws of the Society, but absolutely necessary that, to prevent its falling into improper hands at a remote period, the Warrant should be surrendered forthwith.

""We remain, with fraternal regard, Sir,
"Your very obedient Servants and Brothers, "william H. White,) "edw. Harper, *)* GS

"Mr. John Allen, Lodge 341, Devizes.

—"The contribution of two pounds nine shillings was duly placed to credit of the lodge in the Benevolence Account."

This lodge had been one of the strongest in the Province, and its meetings were for several years very frequent, sometimes as often as four times in the month, and many "makings" of brethren took place; it is therefore singular that thirty years should have elapsed after its dissolution before a new lodge was started. However, in 1856 certain of the brethren of the defunct lodge, with others, petitioned the Grand Lodge for a now Warrant, which was'granted to them under No. 961, subsequently closed up to No. 663.

EXTEACTS FROM THE MINUTE-BOOKS OF THE OLD DEVIZES LODGE. 1792. March 14.—The Provincial Grand Lodge was held at the Saracen's Head Inn, at 11.30, and the W.M. of the lodge was installed. Eight members only, including the Provincial Grand Master, John Dainton, appear to have been present, and the following note is added to the minutes of the meeting:—

"Note.—Five of the brethren were passed, and raised in Lodge No. 170, in his Majesty's 3rd Eegiment of Foot, at their lodge-room, White Hart, Devizes. " 1792. Sept. 11.—The removal of the lodge from the Saracen's Head to the White Hart was agreed to. Initiation of J. Card and L. M. Eogers. 1792. Sept. 14.—At an emergency meeting J. Card and L. M. Eogers were "passed" as "not being residents in the town." 1792. Sept. 25.—At an emergency meeting J. Card and L. M. Rogers were "raised." 1792. Nov. 19.—The removal of the lodge to the Castle Inn was agreed to.

"1793. March 11.—The lodge was not opened on account of the third key being missing." 1793. April 9.—At an emergency meeting Mr. Jones Fish was proposed, "he having been a member before of a modern lodge, and being now desirous to be remade, and to join the Ancients." 1794. April 14.—The meeting of the lodge was postponed to April 16th "on account of a party of the Hereford Militia coming to town, and requ'xing accommodation." 1795. Jan. 12.—Relief was ordered to be given to Brother James Smith, of Lodge of Friendship, South Carolina.

"1795. Aug. 10.—Eegular lodge night, but the Senior Warden being from home with ye key were obliged to adjourn."

"1795. Nov. 9.—Opened in ye third degree, when was granted recommendation to Brother Cooke and Brother Fish to obtain the degree of Holy Arch." 1795. Dec. 14.—Payment of £1 Is. was directed to be made to the Grand Lodge. 1796. March 14.—A resolution was passed to remove the lodge to the White Hart Inn.

"1812. Dec. 18.—Devizes Lodge meeting at Elm Tree Inn."

"1812. Dec. 29.—Brother Gionan Baptista Giobbio admitted as a joining member." 1813. April 13.—A list of members of the lodge was returned to the Grand Lodge.

"Memorandum:—On the 25th November, 1813, the articles of union between the two Grand Lodges of Freemasons were entered into, and on the 1st day of Dec., 1813, the same were ratified and confirmed, and the seals of the two Grand Lodges affixed thereto at the palace at Kensington. The first United Grand Lodge was held on Dec. 27th, 1813."

"1814. June 24.—Capt. Hillier, being in daily expectation of receiving orders to join his regiment, was proposed, approved, and advanced to the first, second, and third steps of Masonry this evening."

"1814. Dec. 9.—The rules, orders, and bye-laws of the Grand Lodge were read." 1815. Feb. 10.—Among the list of visitors are mentioned those of Lodges 523, Frome; 9, East Indies; 53, late 44; 557, Lincoln. In the column "Eank," after the names of visitors, the following different descriptive initials appear, viz. "E.A.," "F.C.," "M.M.," "E. A.M.," "K.T." 1815. Dec. 8.—A fortnightly Lodge of Instruction was agreed upon.

1815. Dec. 27.—A return was made to the Grand Lodge of the 24 members of the lodge. Present amongst the visitors were those of Lodges 509, Berkeley; 557, Lincoln; 524, Newark: 44, Scotch Lodge, "Thistle."

"1816. June 24.—Brother Sampson Samuel, of Lodge 319, attended this lodge, and tendered his services to instruct the brethren in the new system, as agreed on by the Lodge of Eeconciliation, which offer was accordingly adopted."

"1816. June 28.—Brother Thos. Burrough Smith one of the petitioning members in 1856 for the present lodge, and who died in 1879 raised to the third degree according to the new system laid down by the Lodge of Eeconciliation, Brother S. Samuels presiding as Master. " 1817. Feb. 14.—A sword was presented to the lodge by Brother Eeeve, of Birmingham.

1817. March 24.—A report was made of the Provincial Grand Lodge meeting held at Bath, at which 20 members of this lodge had attended.

"1817. May 9.—In consequence of some unforeseen circumstances it was proposed to adjourn the lodge; this was agreed upon on Wednesday last, the 7th instant, by our worthy brother, Mr. Joseph Scott, with whom some of us had a long conversation. Oh! what a change in a few hours, Brother Scott dying suddenly in his chair the same evening. What a lesson to old and young of the uncertainty of this life! Be ye also ready! Little did we expect such a shock when conversing with him in the morning." 1817. Sept. 12.—An invitation was given by Brother Thos. Burrough Smith to the brethren "to attend a lodge at Melksham he was about to open."

"1817. Nov. 27.—A visit was paid to the lodge by the brethren of the Wilts Yeomanry Cavalry, including the W.M. of Lodge 661, of the Five Alls, Salisbury, with his S.W. Brother J. Calley, Esq., M.P. for Cricklade, and others."

"1818. April 12.—Lodge postponed on account of the county election detaining many of the members."

"1818. June 19.—The celebration of St. John's Day agreed to be postponed, on account of the election, until the regular night in July." The W.M. tendered his resignation.

"1818. Nov. 10.—A vote of thanks was passed to the W.M. Brother E. J. Williams (who was absent through illness) for his attention to Masonry, and the good he had done in particular to

Lodge 341." 1821. March 9.—Amongst the visitors was "Brother Withers, W. M. of Swindon Lodge." 1821. Nov. 9.— Eesignation by letter of E. J. Williams as W.M. of the lodge.

1823. July 11.—£8 was received from the Lodge of Benevolence for Brother Buckley. 1826. May 5.—Memorandum of the sale by auction of the lodge furniture, and division of the regalia. EXTEACTS FEOM THE MINUTE-BOOKS OF WILTSHIRE LODGE OF FIDELITY. 1856. April 18.—The lodge was consecrated by Brother D. Gooch, the D.P.G.M.

"1857. April 14.—Brother Simon "Watson Taylor, who had been initiated and passed in 1831 in the Apollo Lodge, Oxford, was raised to the third degree." 1857. Aug. 18.—The Provincial Grand Lodge was received by this lodge.

"1861. June 14.—Eesolved that the Secretary for the time being should be excused his subscription." 1873. March 3.—A meeting was held on the occasion of the funeral of Brother Samuel Wittey, the D.P.G.M., and formerly W. M., and afterwards Secretary of the lodge. The funeral took place with Masonic honours: the members of the Provincial Grand Lodge and a large number of brethren from the various private lodges in the Province attended to pay their last tribute of respect.

1874. Jan. 20.—Installation of the W. M. by Brother Gabriel Goldney, M.P., the D.P.G.M. 1875. March 18.—Notice read of the installation of H.E.H. the Prince of Wales, BIG., as Grand Master at the Eoyal Albert Hall, London, on the 20th April last. LIST OP WORSHIPFUL MASTERS OP

LODGE, No. 341 (formerly 270).

DEVIZES

Tear. Worshipful Master.
1792. E. F. Williams
1793.
1794.
1795.
1796.
1797.

No. of Meetings of the Lodge.
. 16 . 16 . 14 . 12 . 14 . 13

A break occurs here in the minute-book.

2 16 21 15 18 18 14 13 12 12 12 13 12

1 1 LONGLEAT LODGE, No. 1478.

Warrant Dated January 1st, 1874.

Meets At The Town Hall, Warminster.

Lodges Held On Wednesday Nearest The Full Moon

In Each Month, At 7 P.m. Installation Of The W.M. In March. Number Of Members Of The Lodge, 54, Of Whom 4

Are P.M.

LONGLEAT LODGE.

The founders of this lodge were Brothers Lord Henry F. Thynne, M.P., J. V. Toone, G. Pike, E. de M. Lawson, G. H. Bush, S. J. Haden, and W. H. Hardick; and the lodge was consecrated on Friday, February 27th, 1874, the ceremony being performed by D.P.G.M. Brother Gabriel Goldney, M.P., and Brother Terry, Secretary to the Masonic Benevolent Institution for Girls, in the presence of a large number of Provincial Grand Officers and other brethren.

This lodge is largely indebted to Brother Lord Henry F. Thynne, M.P., for its origin; and its continued prosperity and harmony are greatly due to his personal presence and exertions.

EXTRACTS FROM THE MINUTE-BOOK OF LONGLEAT LODGE. 1874. Feb. 27.— Consecration of the lodge, and installation of Brother Lord Henry F. Thynne, M.P., as W.M., by the D.P.G.M., Brother G. Goldney, M.P. 1876. March 10.—H.E.H. Prince Leopold, KG, upon the proposition of E.W. Lord Methuen, P.G.M., seconded by Lord H. F. Thynne, M.P., was elected a joining member without ballot, by special dispensation granted by the Provincial Grand Master. 1876. Nov. 22.—At the Provincial Grand Lodge received by this lodge there were present H.E.H. Prince Leopold and several Grand Masters of other Provinces, and a banner was presented to the Provincial Grand Master, Lord Methuen, by the Wiltshire Brethren. LODGE OF LOYALTY, No. 1533.

Warrant Dated February 13th, 1875.

Meets At The Town Hall, Marlborough.

Lodges Held On Tuesday Nearest The Full Moon

In Every Month, At 5 P.m. Installation Of The W.M. In May. Number Of Members Of The Lodge, 30, Of Whom 3

Are P.M.

LODGE OF LOYALTY.

This lodge was consecrated May 23rd, 1876, by Brother Lord Henry F. Thynne, M.P., Past Grand Warden of England.

LIST OF WOESHIPFUL MASTEES.

No. of Meetings Tear. Worshipful Master. of the Lodge.
1876. JohnToomer 6 1877. Alfred Plummer.... 9 1878. Major Calley 6 1879. John Hammond.... 9 METHUEN LODGE, No. 631.

Warrant Dated 1854.

Meets At Skindle's Hotel, Taflow.

Lodges Held At The End Of May, June, And July. this Lodge Is Now Included In The Province Of Berks And Bucks. METHUEN LODGE.

The 24th of May, 1854, is a memorable day in Wiltshire Masonry, for on that day the imposing ceremony of the consecration of this lodge and the installation of the Provincial Grand Master, Lord Methuen, as its first W.M., was performed in the presence of over five hundred brethren, including many of high Masonic rank. After the conclusion of the ceremony a procession was formed in the following order:— ORDER OF PROCESSION at the Ceremony of laying the Foundation Stone of the Swindon Mechanics' Institution, May 24th, 1854.

Tylers with drawn swords.

Band.

Visiting Brethren, two and two, not Members of Lodges in the Province, and Juniors in rank first.

Lodge of Concord, No. 915.

Methuen Lodge, No. 914.

Lansdowne Lodge of Unity, No. 909.

Elias de Derham Lodge, No. 856.

Royal Sussex Lodge of Emulation, No. 453.

Lodge of Rectitude, No. 420.

A HISTORY OP FREEMASONRY, ETC. 177

Visiting Brethren, two and two, being Provincial Grand Officers of other Provinces, Juniors in rank first.

Builder with Trowel. Architect with Plans.

Cornucopia with Corn, borne by a Master of a Lodge.

Ewer with Wine. Ewer with Oil (each borne by a Master of the Lodge).

Prov. G. Poursuivant. Prov. G. Organist.

Assist. Prov. Gt. Dir. of Ceremonies. Prov. G. Dir. of Ceremonies.

Prov. G. Supt. of Works (with Inscription Plate). Prov. G. Secretary (bearing Book of Constitution on a cushion).' Prov. G. Registrar. Prov. G. Treasurer with Coins. Grand Officers, two and two, Juniors in rank first.

Corinthian Light, borne by a P.M.

Column of Prov. Jun. G. Warden, borne by a M.M.

Prov. Jun. G. Warden with Plumb Rule.

Doric Light, borne by a P.M.

Column of Prov. Sen. G. Warden, borne by a M.M.

Prov. Sen. G. Warden, with Level.

Prov. Jun. G. Deacon.

/ Volume of the Sacred Law
Prov. G. Steward. ʧʧʃSSiEL p-v. G. Steward.

'Prov. Grand Chaplain. /

Deputy Prov. Grand Master with Square.

The Ionic Light, borne by a P.M.

The Mallet, borne by an Officer of Grand Lodge.

Prov. G. Sword Bearer.

Prov. Grand Master.

Prov. Sen. G. Deacon.

Prov. Grand Tyler.

Directors of the Improvement Company, and Council of Institution.

Visitors not Masons, two and two.

Ancient Order of Foresters, two and two.

Manchester Unity of Odd Fellows, two and two.

The brethren proceeded to St. Mark's Church, where divine service was held, and the new stained-glass western window was uncovered for the first time. The procession was then reformed, and went to the Market Place, where the foundation-stone of the new Mechanics' Institution was laid, with the usual

Masonic rites, by Lord Methuen, assisted by his officers.

In 1869, upon Sir Daniel Gooch being appointed Provincial Grand Master for Berks and Bucks, this lodge was by arrangement transferred to that Province.

EXTRACTS FEOM THE MINUTE-BOOK OF METHUEN LODGE.

"1854. May 24.—At the first regular meeting of the lodge the following brethren were present:—

Lord Methuen, E.W. Prov. Grand Master for Wilts.

Sir Watkin W. Wynn, E.W. Prov. Grand Master for
North Wales and Shropshire.

D. Gooch, Dep. Prov. Grand Master for Wilts.

— Bisgood,,,,, for Kent.

— Huyshe, ,, ,, for Devon.

— Nash, ,,,, for Bristol.

— Stone, P.G.W.

— Eowe, P.G.D.

— Hervey, P.G.D.

and about 500 Provincial Grand Officers and Brethren."

"Brother D. Gooch, Dep. Provincial Grand Master for Wilts, having taken the chair as W.M., proceeded to consecrate, dedicate, and constitute the Methuen Lodge according to the ancient rites and ceremonies of our venerable Order, after which Brother Hervey, G.D., presented the Eight Hon. Lord Methuen, P.G.M., for installation as W. M. of the Methuen Lodge, whereupon he was duly installed according to the ancient form by Brother D. Gooch, in the presence of ninety installed masters.

"All business being ended, the lodge was closed, and the E.W. Provincial Grand Master immediately opened his Provincial Grand Lodge, and then proceeded to St. Mark's Church, where divine service was performed, and the new stained-glass western window was uncovered; after which his lordship laid the foundation-stone of the new Swindon Mechanics' Institution with Masonic rites, and having returned to the lodge-room and closed the Grand Lodge, the brethren retired to the banquet." 1856. Sept. 10.—The Provincial Grand Lodge was received by this lodge.

1857. May 6.—A sword was presented by Brother Cammell to the lodge. 1863. Sept. 16.—A letter was read from the Grand Lodge stating that the number of this lodge would in future be moved up from 914 to 631. 1869. July 8.—The question of the removal of the lodge, and the steps that had been taken as to the same, and the formation of a new lodge, to be called the Gooch Lodge, and to be held at the Queen's Eoyal Hotel, New Swindon, having been fully discussed, as also the propriety of making over the heavier furniture to the new lodge, "it was unanimously resolved that the lodge be removed to Maidenhead, in the Province of Berks and Bucks, subject to the consent of the Provincial Grand Masters of Wilts, and Berks and Bucks, and that every assistance be given by this lodge to the promotion of the Gooch Lodge by a loan of its furniture or otherwise."

"1870. May 7.—Orkney Arms, Maidenhead. The E.W.P.G.M. for Berks and Bucks (Sir D. Gooch, Bart. , M.P.), announced to the lodge that all the formalities for the removal of the lodge had been complied with, and the certificates from himself and the Provincial Grand Master for Wilts given for the removal to Maidenhead. With reference to the furniture and jewels belonging to the lodge, and now at Swindon, the W.M. undertook to forward an inventory of them, and it was deputed to Brother Eoberts to direct that all he thought proper should be sent to Maidenhead, and to present to the Gooch Lodge the heavy furniture." LIST OF WOESHIPFUL MASTEES OF METHUEN LODGE.

Year. Worshipful Master.
1854. Lord Methuen, P.G.M. 1855. Francis 0. Hodgkinson. 1856. Edward Roberts.
1857. S. Dunning.
1858. Sir Daniel Gooch, Bart., M.P. 1859. Thomas E. M. Marsh. 1860. William F. Gooch. 1861. Major John Elton Merion Prower. 1862. E. Benham. 1863. William Martley.
1864.
1865. William C. Merriman. 1866. „ „ „

1867. Edward A. Moore. 1868. 0. Cammell. 1869. Henry Kinneir. 1870. The lodge left the Province of Wiltshire. WILTSHIRE PROVINCIAL GRAND CHAPTER OF ROYAL ARCH MASONS.

As far as can be ascertained Royal Arch Masonry took but little bold in this County until quite recently.

In 1797 Most Excellent Companion Micbael Burrough, of SaHsbury (the writer's great-grandfather), was Grand Superintendent for the Province of Wiltshire (as well as Grand Master of Knight-Templars, &c, &c), and there appear to have been then two chapters in Wiltshire, numbered 20 and 31, but without any distinctive names. No particulars of these chapters have been found beyond incidental mention of them, and they apparently ceased a few years after that date.

The next Provincial Grand Superintendent we hear of was Most Excellent Companion Samuel Wittey, of Devizes, who was appointed in 1870, but died three years afterwards; and the office was vacant until Most Excellent Companion the Eight Hon. Lord Henry F. Thynne, M.P., was appointed in 1875, who by his excellent administration has brought Eoyal Arch Masonry into high repute in the Province.

A HISTORY OF FREEMASONRY, ETC. 188

At present there are three chapters, namely, Elias de Derham, No. 586, held at Salisbury; Wiltshire Chapter, attached to the Eoyal Sussex Lodge of Emulation, No. 355, held at Swindon; and Chapter of Harmony, No. 632, held at Trowbridge; but it is hoped that before long there will be one established at Chippenham and other important towns.

At the time the present Provincial Grand Superintendent was appointed, there were sixty-five companions in the Province; there are now seventy-three, and further additions will no doubt soon be made to their number.

The Provincial Grand Chapter meets once a year in the autumn, in the town of the three chapters in turns.

On the occasion of the resuscitation of the Provincial Grand Chapter, and the installation of Most Excellent Com-

panion Lord H. F. Thynne, at Swindon, on the 3rd of September, 1875, the Eight Worshipful Provincial Grand Master, Lord Methuen, then Provincial Grand H. Wilts, dedicated the new Masonic Hall in Victoria Street to the uses of the craft.

1870. June 6. Af a meeting of Wiltshire Chapter, No. 335, held at Swindon, the Patent was read appointing Ex. Comp. Samuel Wittey (who was M.E.Z. of that Chapter) to be the Provincial Grand Superintendent of Eoyal Arch Masons in and over Wiltshire, and he was afterwards duly installed by Most Excellent Companion John Henry, G.S.E.

A resolution was unanimously passed that "an uniform plan for the working of the several Chapters in the Province should be adopted." 1871. Oct. 6. The Provincial Grand Chapter met at Salisbury, where they were received by the present and past Principals, Officers, and Companions of Chapter of Harmony, No. 632.

1872. Oct. 11. The Provincial Grand Chapter met at Trowbridge. The report of the Committee which had been appointed for determining upon the Eitual was brought up and adopted, and ordered to be submitted the Grand Scribe E. for his approval. 1875. Sept. 3. The Provincial Grand Chapter met at Swindon, when it was announced that the Most Excellent Grand Z. of England, H. E.H. the Prince of Wales, had appointed Most Ex. Comp., the Eight Hon. Lord Henry F. Thynne, M.P., to the office of Provincial Grand Superintendent for Wiltshire, which had become vacant by the death of Most Ex. Comp. Wittey.

The following Patent was read by Ex. Comp. Henry C. Tombs, the Provincial Grand Scribe E..

Albert Edward, Z. "Carnarvon, H. Warren D. Tabjuey, J.

"To all and every our Most Excellent and Excellent Companions of the Sublime Degree of Eoyal Arch Masons Health, Peace, Goodwill..

381® % Post fetlltnt % (grano principals having taken into our consideration the constant care of our Excellent Companion Lord Henry Frederick Thynne for the Honour of the Society and his zealous endeavours to promote the First Principles of the Institution, and being desirous ourselves to the best of our Power to render his labours effectual, have thought it expedient for that purpose to appoint, and by tis our sKarratti of Commission do appoint, our said Excellent Companion %t $igfct f)o curable 'garb ienrjr jKforirk ftbjmu, $.$., to be our Post feulkni Snpmrftnbtni in and over the)robiitce of sHittsjjiu. And we the said *Grand Principals* do hereby require our said Most Excellent and Grand Superintendent Lord Henry Frederick Thynne at all convenient times and places within the said Province to examine into the state of the several *Chapters* of the *Order,* to inspect their Customs and Practices, and in cases where necessary to advise, instruct, and admonish, as to *you* may seem meet, *keeping always in view* the true intent and meaning of the laws established for the Government of the Masonic Society in general, and of our *Most Supreme Degree* in particular.

"Given at London under our hands and the Seal of our (gratrfc and frugal dtjjapttr this 11th day of March, A.Z. 5875, A.D. 1875.

"Henry F. Thynne, N. "John Hervey, E."

Lord Henry F. Thynne, M.P., was then installed by Most Ex. Comp. John Hervey, G.S.E., after which he appointed Ex. Comp. the Eight Hon. Lord Methuen to be Provincial Grand H., and Ex. Comp. E. Bradford to be Provincial Grand J., and they and the other Provincial Grand Officers were duly invested with the collars and jewels of their respective offices.

The Companions of Elias de Derham Chapter presented the jewel of a P.Z. to the Provincial Grand Superintendent, who was a member of their Chapter.

Ex. Comp. Henry C. Tombs called attention to the formation of a Provincial Grand Charity Organization Committee, and the Provincial Grand Treasurer was consequently directed to attend the meeting of such Committee as the representative of the Provincial Grand Chapter.

The Companions subsequently ad-journed to the banquet, which was attended by a large number of distinguished Masons of this and adjoining Provinces, and where the health of the Provincial Grand Superintendent, Lord Henry F. Thynne, M.P., was proposed in felicitous terms by the Eight Hon. Lord Methuen, and was received hy the Companions with enthusiasm.

1876. August 2. At the Meeting of the Provincial Grand Chapter held at Salisbury there were present a great number of distinguished Companions from this Province, and also from London and the Provinces of Dorset, Berks and Bucks, Gloucester, Somerset, and Oxford, including—

Most Ex. Comp. H.E.H. Prince Leopold, P.G.M. Oxon. „ „ Eight Hon. Lord Methuen, P.G.H. Wilts. „ „ W. W. B. Beach, P.G.S. Hampshire and Isle of Wight.„„ John Hervey, G. S.E. Ex. Comp. A. H. Hood, 345.„ E. Collins, Apollo.

"After the Provincial Grand Chapter had been opened in ample form, the Provincial Grand Superintendent rose and expressed the great pleasure it afforded him and the Provincial Grand Chapter to welcome Most Ex. Comp. H. E.H. Prince Leopold.

"It was a bright day for Eoyal Arch Masonry in this Province to see it patronised by so distinguished and beloved a member of the Eoyal Family, who had lately taken up his residence amongst Wiltshiremen. He was firmly convinced that the Companions duly appreciated the honour paid to them, and that they hoped that his Eoyal Highness would feel assured that come amongst them whenever he might, the Province would be found carrying out, in the strictest and most Masonic manner, the Laws and Eegulations prescribed by the Grand Chapter of England, and therefore at all times prepared for the inspection of their illustrious visitor or any other Companion of distinction who might honour them with a visit.

1877. July 20. At a meeting of the Provincial Grand Chapter at Trowbridge, the retirement of Ex. Comp. E. Bradford from the office of Provincial Grand Treasurer on account of ill-health was announced, and received with regret; and after a cordial vote of thanks had been passed to him for his past services, Ex. Comp. W. Nott was elected in his place. 1878. August 9.—At a meeting of the Provincial Grand Chapter at Swindon, Sir D. Gooch, Bart., M.P., Most Ex. Superintendent for Berks and Bucks, was present, and his services to this Province, of which he was the oldest P.Z., were feelingly alluded to by the Provincial Grand Superintendent. 1879. August 22.—At a meeting at Salisbury the Provincial Grand Superintendent informed the Companions that for the future the Provincial Grand Chapter would be opened in strict form as an independent Chapter, and not be "received" by a Chapter as heretofore.

Amongst the distinguished visitors present was Most Ex. Comp. J. M. P. Montague, Provincial Grand Superintendent of Dorsetshire.

A vote of thanks was unanimously passed to Ex. Comp. Thos. Graham, Superintendent of the Great Western Eailway at Bristol, upon his retirement from that office, for his courteous and ready assistance to the Companions in affording them facilities for travelling on the occasions of all Provincial Grand Chapter Meetings since the establishment of the Provincial Grand Chapter. EOLL OF OFFICERS OF THE EOYAL AECH PEOVINCIAL GEAND CHAPTER.

MOST EXCELLENT SUPERINTENDENT.

1797. Michael Bin-rough.
1870. Samuel Wittey.
1875. Eight Hon. Lord Henry F. Thynne, M.P.
EX. P.G.H. 1870. Thomas Chandler. 1871. R. de M. Lawson. 1872. William Bead. 1873-4. P.G. Chapter in abeyance. 1875. Right Hon. Lord Methuen. 1876. Horatio Ward. 1877. John Chandler. 1878. Richard Bradford. 1879. JohnToomer. EX. P.G.J. 1870. John Chandler. 1871. Henry Kinneir. 1872. John Toomer. 1873-4. P.G. Chapter in abeyance 1875. Richard Bradford. 1876. Frederick King. 1877. Rohert Stokes. 1878. JohnToomer. 1879. Thos. F. Eavenshaw. EX. P.G.S.E. 1870. Henry C. Tombs. 1871. 1872. 1873-4. P.

G. Chapter in abeyance. 1875. Henry C. Tombs. 1876. ,, 1877. ,,
1878.
1879.
P.G.S.N.
1870. Henry Kinneir. 1871. C. W. Wyndham. 1872. Horatio Ward. 1873-4. P. G. Chapter in abeyance. 1875. Frederick King. 1876. Henry Calley. 1877. James Sparks. 1878. None. 1879. Thos. S. Futcher.
P.G.P.S.
1870. E. de M. Lawson. 1871. Robert Stokes. 1872. Frederick King. 1873-4. P.G. Chapter in abeyance. 1875. Alexander J. Braid. 1876. Thomas Prideaux Saun ders. 1877. Thomas S. Futcher. 1878. None. 1879. Thomas P. Saunders. 1st ASSIST. SOJE. 1870. C. W. Wyndham. 1871. Frederick King, _«» 1872. Richard Tarrant. 1873-4. P.G. Chapter in abeyance. 1875. Henry Calley. 1876. Samuel Gauntlett. 1877. None. 1878. ,, 1879. John Rumbold. 2nd ASSIST. SOJR. 1870. Robert Stokes. 1871. H. P. Blaekmore. 1872. S. Gauntlett. 1873-4. P.G. Chapter in abeyance. 1875. Joseph J. New. 1876. William Nott. 1877. None. ,, 1878. ,, 1879. ,, TREASURER. 1870. Richard Bradford. 1871. 1872. 1873-4. P.G. Chapter in abeyance. 1875. Richard Bradford. 1876. ,, 1877. William Nott. 1878.
1879. REGISTRAR. 1870. William Read. 1871. William Nott.
1872.
1873-4. P.G. Chapter in abeyance. 1875. 1876. John Toomer. 1877. S. H. Perman. 1878. Thomas Newbury. 1879. Alfred Plummer. SWORD BEARER. 1870. Sidney Perman. 1871. ,, 1872. T. P. Saunders. 1873-4. P.G. Chapter in abeyance. 1875. John Chandler. 1876. S. H. Perman. 1877. Alfred Plummer. 1878. John Rumbold. 1879. None. STANDARD BEARER. 1871. Noah Rogers. 1872. Joseph Wentworth. 1873-4. P.G Chapter in abeyance. 1875. William Read. 1876. None. 1877. ,, 1878. ,, 1879. ,, DIRECTOR OF CERE-
MONIES.
1870. Horatio Ward.
1871.
1872. James Sparks. 1873-4. P.G.

Chapter in abeyance. 1875. Horatio Ward. 1876. Richard Tarrant. 1877. T. P. Saunders. 1878. John Chandler. 1879. ,, ORGANIST. 1871. James Sparks. 1872. Richard Bowly. 1873-4. P.G. Chapter in abeyance.
1875. James Sparks.
1876. ,, 1877. None. 1878. ,, 1879. ,, STEWARD. 1870. Joseph Burt.
,, E. R. Ing.
,, Richard Tarrant. 1871 —Gray.
,, — Saxty.
,, T. P. Saunders. 1872. William Westmacott.
,, J. R. Shopland.
,, Alfred Plummer. 1873-4. P.G. Chapter in abeyance.

LIST OF CHAPTERS WOEKING AT THE PEESENT TIME IN THE PEOVINCE OP WILTSHIEE.
WILTSHIRE CHAPTER, No. 355.
ELIAS DE DERHAM CHAPTER, No. 586.
CHAPTER OF HARMONY, No. 632.
WILTSHIRE CHAPTER, No. 355.
Warrant Dated February 6th, 1856.
Meets At The Masonic Hall, Swindon.
Chapters Held On Friday Nearest The Full Moon
In January, February, October, November,
And December, At 4 P.m. Installation Of Principals On St. John's Day In The
Month Of December. Number Of Members Of The Chapter, 29, Of Whom 11
Are P.Z.

WILTSHIEE CHAPTER.
This Chapter was founded in 1856 by Excellent Companions Sir Daniel Gooch, Bart., M.P., J. W. Browne, Henry Weaver, and others, and was consecrated by Excellent Companion Levean, P.G.D.C.
LIST OF EXCELLENT Z.
Year.
1856. 18S7. 1858. 1859. 1860. 1861. 1862. 1863. 1864. 1865. 1866. 1867. 1868. 1869. 1870. 1871. 1872. 1873. 1874. 1875. 1876. 1877. 1878. 1879.
Excellent Z. Sir Daniel Gooch, Bart., M.P.
J. W. Browne.
"William F. Gooch
»»» »»»

Col. Thomas Goddard
Thomas Chandler
John Chandler.
Richard Bradford
» »
William Read.
R. de M. Lawson
John Toomer
Samuel Wittey.
Henry Kinneir.
Joseph Wentworth
Richard Tarrant
A. J. Braid
Henry C. Tombs
Rt. Hon. Lord Methuen
John Chandler.
J. J. New.
Alfred Plummer
No. of Meetings of the Chapter.
3 2 2 3 3 2 1 5 5 4 3 5 3 4 5 4 3 4 5 6 4 3 5 4 ELIAS DE DEEHAM CHAPTER, No. 586.
Warrant Dated August 7th, 1867.
Meets At The Masonic Hall, Salisbury.
Chapters Held On The Third Friday In January,
March, August, September, And November, At
7 P.m.
Installation Of The Principals On The Third Friday
In September. Number Members Of The Chapter, 28, Of Whom 4
Are P.Z.
ELIAS DE DERHAM CHAPTER.
The Chapter was consecrated 31st October, 1867, by the Eight Worshipful and Most Excellent Companion Joseph Gundry, Provincial Grand Superintendent of Dorset.
LIST OF EXCELLENT Z.
No. of Meetings Year. Excellent Z. of the Chapter, 1867. Rev. Frederick King. ... 5 1868. Rev. Wm. Mortimer Heath. . 5 1869. Charles Wadham Wyndham.. 4 1870. Robert Stokes 5 1871. Horatio Ward 4 1872. ,, 2 1873. Humphrey P. Blackmore... 6 1874. Lord Henry F. Thynne, M.P... 5 1875. S. H. Perman 3 1876. John Newbery 4 1877. Thos. S. Futcher.... 5 1878. John Rumbold 5 1879. Francis Jeffery Russell... 4 CHAPTER OF HAEMONY, No.-632.
Warrant Dated May 5th, 1869.
Meets At The Masonic Hall, Trow-

bridge.

Chapters Held On The Third "wednesday In The Months Of January, March, May, September, And November, At 6 O'clock P.m.

Installation Of Principals In September.

Number Of Members Of The Chapter, 16, Of Whom 7 Are P.Z.

CHAPTER OF HARMONY.

This Chapter was consecrated on Sept. 15th, 1869, by the Provincial Companion Joseph Gundry, Eight Worshipful and Most Excellent Grand Superintendent of Dorset.

EXTEACTS FEOM THE MINUTE-BOOK OF CHAPTER OF HARMONY. 1869. Sept. 29.

—A vote of thanks was passed to Comp. H. Ward for his gift of a set of robes; also to Comp. S. Wittey for his gift of a set of surplices. 1870. Sept. 21. —It was unanimously agreed that the thanks of the Chapter be given to Comp. E. de M. Lawson for his valuable and gratuitous work in the furnishing of the Chapter, now supplemented by the gift of the banners, and that a P.Z. jewel be presented to him in testimony of the same. 1872. Oct. 11.—The Provincial Grand Chapter was received by this Chapter. 1873. March 19.—A,vote expressing the condolence of the Chapter with Mrs. Wittey, widow of the late M. E. Comp. Wittey, Provincial Grand Superintendent of the Province, was passed. 1875. March 22.—A petition was signed for the appointment of the Most Excellent Comp. Lord Henry F. Thynne, G.N., as Provincial Grand Superintendent for Wiltshire. LIST OF EXCELLENT Z.

Year. Excellent Z.

1869. R. de M. Lawson 1870. F. J F. Ravenshaw. 1871. John Gray. 1872. William Nott. 1873. Samuel Gauntlet 1874. Thomas Prideaux Saunders 1875. F. Vere Holloway. 1876. Henry Richardson 1877. James Sparks. 1878. ,, ,, ".. 1879.,

No. of Meetings of the Chapter.

4. 5. 4. 5. 4. 5. 5. 4. 5 4. 5. 3. 3

CPSIA information can be obtained at www.ICGtesting.com
Printed in the USA
BVOW06s1148050114

340869BV00005B/97/P